Assessment Manual PowerPoint 2002

Comprehensive

Margaret Marple

Glencoe McGraw-Hill

New York, New York Columbus, Ohio Chicago, Illinois Peoria, Illinois Woodland Hills, California

This program has been prepared with the assistance of Gleason Group, Inc., Norwalk, CT.

Editorial Director: Pamela Ross
Project Manager: Marilyn Jean Young
Composition: CFM Designs

A Division of The McGraw-Hill Companies

PowerPoint 2002, Comprehensive
Assessment Manual

1 2 3 4 5 6 7 8 9 10 024 07 06 05 04 03 02

ISBN 0-07-827972-0

Contents

ExamView Pro Test Generator

SECTION 1 — INTRODUCTION

This user's guide accompanies a test generator program called *ExamView® Pro 3.0*–an application that enables you to quickly create printed tests, Internet tests, and computer (LAN-based) tests. You can enter your own questions and customize the appearance of the tests you create. The *ExamView Pro* test generator program offers many unique features. Using the QuickTest wizard, for example, you are guided step-by-step through the process of building a test. Numerous options are included that allow you to customize the content and appearance of the tests you create.

As you work with the *ExamView* test generator, you may use the following features:

- **an interview mode or "wizard" to guide you through the steps to create a test in less than five minutes**
- **five methods to select test questions**
  - random selection
  - from a list
  - while viewing questions
  - by criteria (difficulty code, objective, topic, etc.–if available)
  - all questions
- **the capability to edit questions or to add an unlimited number of questions**
- **online (*Internet-based*) testing**
  - create a test that students can take on the Internet using a browser
  - receive instant feedback via email
  - create online study guides with student feedback for incorrect responses
  - include any of the twelve (12) question types
- **Internet test-hosting** *
  - instantly publish a test to the *ExamView* website
  - manage tests online
  - allow students to access tests from one convenient location
  - receive detailed reports
  - download results to your gradebook or spreadsheet
- **online (*LAN-based*) testing**
  - allow anyone or selected students to take a test on your local area network
  - schedule tests
  - create online study guides with student feedback for incorrect responses
  - incorporate multimedia links (movies and audio)
  - export student results to a gradebook or spreadsheet
- **a sophisticated word processor**
  - streamlined question entry with spell checker
  - tabs, fonts, symbols, foreign characters, and text styles
  - tables with borders and shading
  - full-featured equation editor
  - pictures or other graphics within a question, answer, or narrative
- **numerous test layout and printing options**
  - scramble the choices in multiple choice questions
  - print multiple versions of the same test with corresponding answer keys
  - print an answer key strip for easier test grading
- **link groups of questions to common narratives**

* The Internet test-hosting service must be purchased separately. Visit www.examview.com to learn more.

SECTION 2 — INSTALLATION AND STARTUP INSTRUCTIONS

The *ExamView Pro 3.0* test generator software is provided on a CD-ROM or floppy disks. The disc includes the program and all of the questions for the corresponding textbook. The *ExamView Test Player,* which can be used by your students to take online (computerized or LAN-based) tests, is also included.

Before you can use the test generator, you must install it on your hard drive. The system requirements, installation instructions, and startup procedures are provided below.

SYSTEM REQUIREMENTS

To use the *ExamView Pro 3.0* test generator or the online test player, your computer must meet or exceed the following minimum hardware requirements:

Windows

- Pentium computer
- Windows 95, Windows 98, Windows 2000 (or a more recent version)
- color monitor (VGA-compatible)
- CD-ROM and/or high-density floppy disk drive
- hard drive with at least 7 MB space available
- 8 MB available memory *(16 MB memory recommended)*
- an Internet connection to access the Internet test-hosting features

Macintosh

- PowerPC processor, 100 MHz computer
- System 7.5 (or a more recent version)
- color monitor (VGA-compatible)
- CD-ROM and/or high-density floppy disk drive
- hard drive with at least 7 MB space available
- 8 MB available memory *(16 MB memory recommended)*
- an Internet connection with System 8.6 (or more recent version) to access the Internet test-hosting features

INSTALLATION INSTRUCTIONS

Follow these steps to install the *ExamView* test generator software. The setup program will automatically install everything you need to use *ExamView.* **Note:** A separate test player setup program is also included for your convenience. [See *Online (LAN-based) Testing* on page 9 for more information.]

Windows

Step 1
Turn on your computer.

Step 2
Insert the *ExamView* disc into the CD-ROM drive. If the program is provided on floppy disks, insert Disk 1 into Drive A.

Step 3
Click the **Start** button on the *Taskbar* and choose the *Run* option.

Step 4
If the *ExamView* software is provided on a CD-ROM, use the drive letter that corresponds to the CD-ROM drive on your computer (e.g., **d:\setup.exe**). The setup program, however, may be located in a subfolder on the CD-ROM if the *ExamView* software is included on the disc with other resources. In which case, click the **Browse** button in the Run dialog box to locate the setup program (e.g., **d:\evpro\setup.exe**).

If you are installing the software from floppy disks, type **a:\setup** and press **Enter** to run the installation program.

Step 5
Follow the prompts on the screen to complete the installation process.

If the software and question banks are provided on more than one floppy disk, you will be prompted to insert the appropriate disk when it is needed.

Step 6
Remove the installation disc when you finish.

Macintosh

Step 1
Turn on your computer.

Step 2
Insert the *ExamView* installation disc into your CD-ROM drive. If the program is provided on floppy disks, insert Disk 1 into a disk drive.

Step 3
Open the installer window, if necessary.

Step 4
Double-click the installation icon to start the program.

Step 5
Follow the prompts on the screen to complete the installation process.

If the software and question banks are provided on more than one floppy disk, you will be prompted to insert the appropriate disk when it is needed.

Step 6
Remove the installation disc when you finish.

GETTING STARTED

After you complete the installation process, follow these instructions to start the *ExamView* test generator software. This section also explains the options used to create a test and edit a question bank.

Startup Instructions

Step 1
Turn on the computer.

Step 2

Windows: Click the **Start** button on the *Taskbar.* Highlight the **Programs** menu and locate the *ExamView Test Generator* folder. Select the *ExamView Pro* option to start the software.

Macintosh: Locate and open the *ExamView* folder. Double-click the *ExamView Pro* program icon.

Step 3
The first time you run the software, you will be prompted to enter your name, school/institution name, and city/state. You are now ready to begin using the *ExamView* software.

Step 4
Each time you start *ExamView,* the **Startup** menu appears. Choose one of the options shown in Figure 1. **Note:** All of the figures shown in this user's guide are taken from the Windows software. Except for a few minor differences, the Macintosh screens are identical.

Step 5
Use *ExamView* to create a test or edit questions in a question bank.

ExamView includes three components: Test Builder, Question Bank Editor, and Test Player. The **Test Builder** includes options to create, edit, print, and save tests. The **Question Bank Editor** lets you create or edit question banks. The **Test Player** is a separate program that your students can use to take online (LAN-based) tests/study guides.

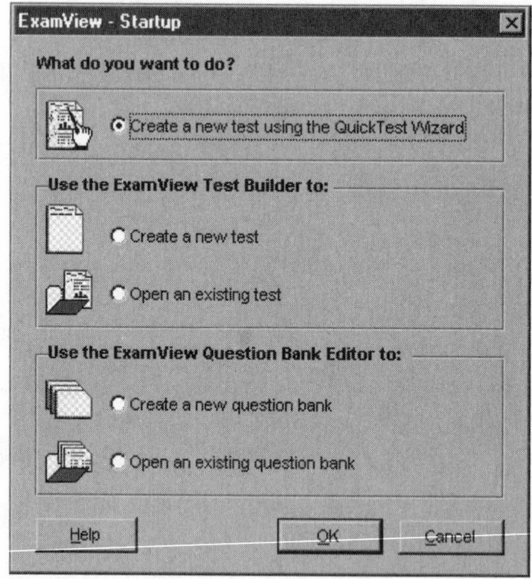

Figure 1 – ExamView Startup Menu

Using The Help System

Whenever you need assistance using *ExamView,* access the extensive help system. Click the **Help** button or choose the **Help Topics** option from the *Help* menu to access step-by-step instructions from more than 150 help topics. If you experience any difficulties while you are working with the software, you may want to review the troubleshooting tips in the user-friendly help system.

Test Builder

The Test Builder allows you to create tests using the QuickTest Wizard, or you can create a new test on your own. (See the sample test in Figure 2.) Use the Test Builder to prepare both printed and online tests/study guides.

- ***If you want ExamView to select questions randomly from one or more question banks,*** choose the *QuickTest Wizard* option to create a new test. (Refer to Figure 1 on page 4.) Then, follow the step-by-step instructions to (1) enter a test title, (2) choose one or more question banks from which to select questions, and (3) identify how many questions you want on the test. The QuickTest Wizard will automatically create a new test and use the Test Builder to display the test on screen. You can print the test as is, remove questions, add new questions, or edit any question.
- ***If you want to create a new test on your own,*** choose the option to create a new test. (Refer to Figure 1 on page 4.) Then, identify a question bank from which to choose questions by using the *Question Bank* option in the **Select** menu. You may then add questions to the test by using one or more of the following selection options: *Randomly, From a List, While Viewing, By Criteria,* or *All Questions.*

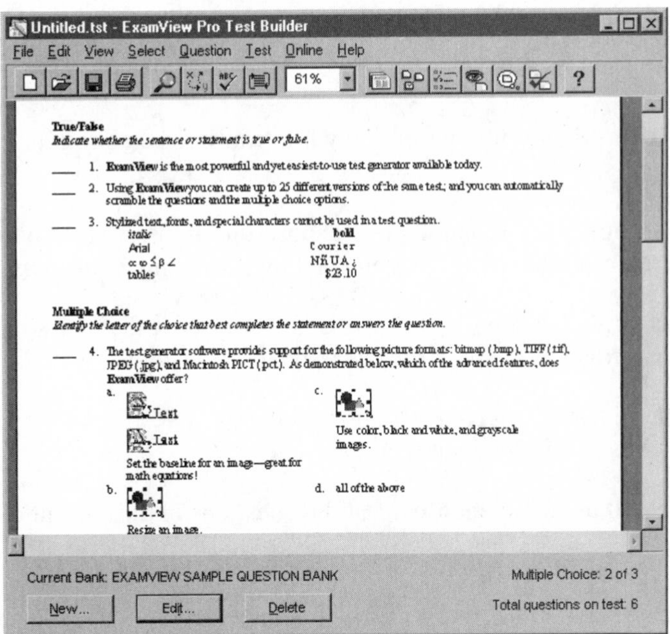

Figure 2 – Sample Test

IMPORTANT: The Test Builder and the Question Bank Editor systems are integrated in one program. As you work with *ExamView*, you can easily switch between the Test Builder and Question Bank Editor components using the *Switch to...* option in the **File** menu.

To create a new test:

Step 1
Start the *ExamView* software.

Step 2
At the Startup window, choose the *Create a new test* option.

Step 3
Enter a title for the new test.

After you enter the title, the program will automatically display the option for you to select a question bank.

Step 4
Choose a question bank.

Step 5
Select the questions you want to include on the test.

Use the question selection options that appear in the **Select** menu. Or, click the corresponding buttons on the toolbar. A description for each of the question selection toolbar buttons appears below.

Click the **Question Bank** toolbar button to select a question bank.

You can create a test using questions from one question bank or from multiple banks. Choose a bank, select the questions you want, and then choose another bank to select more questions.

Click the **Select Randomly** toolbar button when you want the program to randomly select questions for you.

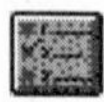
Use the **Select from a List** command to choose questions if you know which ones you want to select. Identify the questions you want by reviewing a question bank printout.

Click the **Select while Viewing** button to display a window that shows all of the questions in the current question bank. Click the check boxes to select the questions you want.

You can use the **Select by Criteria** option to choose questions based on question type, difficulty, and objective (if available).

Click the **Select All** button to choose all of the questions in the current question bank.

Step 6
Save the test.

Step 7
Print the test.

You can use the options in the **Test** menu to customize the appearance of a test, edit test instructions, and choose to leave space for students to write their answers. When you print a test, you may choose how many variations of the test you want, whether you want all the versions to be the same, and whether you want to scramble the questions and the multiple choice options. If you choose to scramble the questions, *ExamView* will print a custom answer sheet for each variation of the test.

If you want your students to take a test online, first create the test. Then, publish the test as an Internet test/study guide (page 15) or use the Online Test Wizard (page 10) to create a test for delivery over a LAN (local area network). The software will walk you through the steps to turn any test into an online (Internet or LAN-based) test.

IMPORTANT: You may edit questions or create new questions as you build your test. However, those questions can be used only as part of the current test. If you plan to create several new questions that you would like to use on other tests, switch to the Question Bank Editor to add the new questions.

Question Bank Editor

The Question Bank Editor allows you to edit questions in an existing publisher-supplied question bank or to create your own new question banks. Always use the Question Bank Editor if you want to change a question permanently in an existing question bank. If you want to make a change that applies only to a particular test, create a new question or edit that question in the Test Builder.

A question bank may include up to 250 questions in a variety of formats including multiple choice, true/false, modified true/false, completion, yes/no, matching, problem, essay, short answer, case, and numeric response. You can include the following information for each question: difficulty code, reference, text objective, state objectives, topic, and notes.

Step 1
Start the *ExamView* software.

Step 2
At the Startup window as illustrated in Figure 1 on page 4, choose to *Create a new question bank* or *Open an existing question bank.*

If you are working in the Test Builder, click the **File** menu and choose *Switch to Question Bank Editor* to edit or create a new question bank.

Step 3
Click the **New** button to create a new question or click the **Edit** button to modify an existing question. Both of these buttons appear at the bottom of the Question Bank Editor window. (See Figure 3.)

You may add new questions or edit questions in a question bank by using the built-in word processor. The word processor includes many features commonly found in commercially available word processing applications. These features include the following: fonts, styles, tables, paragraph formatting, ruler controls, tabs, indents, and justification.

Step 4
Save your work. Then, exit the program or switch back to the Test Builder.

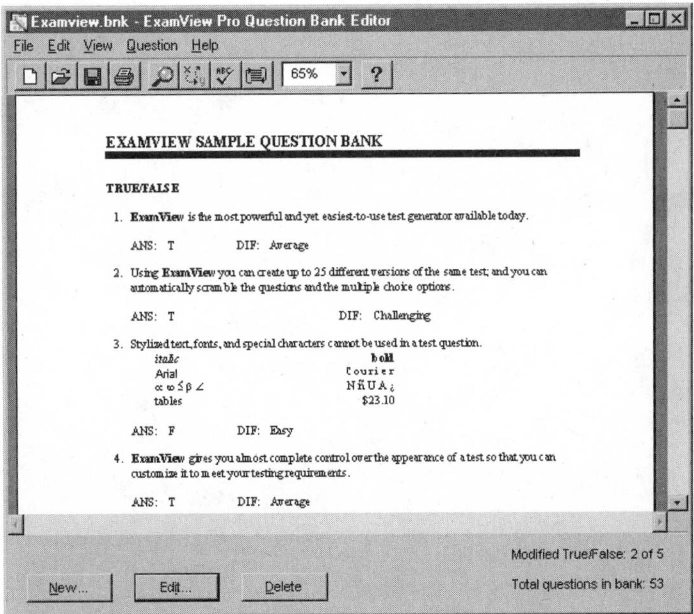

Figure 3 – Question Bank Editor

Online Testing (LAN-based vs. Internet)

The *ExamView* software allows you to create paper tests and online tests. The program provides two distinct online testing options: **LAN-based** testing and **Internet** testing. The option you choose depends on your particular testing needs. You can choose either option to administer online tests and study guides.

The **LAN-based** testing option is designed to work on a local area network server. That is, you can copy the test/study guide along with the Test Player software onto your local area network. Then students can take the test at computers connected to your server.

To take a LAN-based test, you must provide access for your students to the Test Player program included with the *ExamView* software. The Test Player is a separate program that lets your students take a test/study guide at a computer. You can store the Test Player program and the test on a local area network for easy access by your students.

The **Internet** testing option provides a computerized testing solution for delivering tests via the Internet or an Intranet. This option is great for distance learning environments or simply to make a sample test/study guide available to students at home. Students do not need any other program (unlike the LAN-based option). When your students take a test, the results are automatically sent to you via email.

You can publish an Internet test to your own website, or you can use the *ExamView* Internet test-hosting service. If you subscribe to the *ExamView* test-hosting service, you can publish a test directly to the Internet with just a few simple steps. Students will have immediate access to the tests that you publish and you can get detailed reports. For more information on the Internet test-hosting service, visit our website at www.examview.com.

SECTION 3 — ONLINE (LAN-BASED) TESTING

Online testing features are seamlessly integrated into the *ExamView* software. If you want to take advantage of these capabilities, simply create a test and then use the Online Test Wizard to set up the testing parameters. Students can then take the test at the computer using the Test Player program.

IMPORTANT: If you want to prepare a test/study guide for delivery via the Internet, use the *Publish Internet Test* option as described on page 16.

ExamView includes many features that let you customize an online (LAN-based) test. You can create a test for a specific class, or you can prepare a study guide for anyone to take. Using the Online Test Wizard, you can schedule a test or allow it to be taken anytime. As your students work on a test, *ExamView* will scramble the question order, provide feedback for incorrect responses, and display a timer if you selected any of these options.

ONLINE (LAN-BASED) TESTING OVERVIEW

Refer to the steps below for an overview of the online (LAN-based) testing process. Specific instructions for creating a test, taking a test, and viewing results are provided on the following pages.

Step 1
Talk with your network administrator to help you set up a location (folder) on your local area network where you can install the Test Player software and copy your tests/study guides.

Make sure that the administrator gives you and your students full access to the designated folders on the server. You may also want your network administrator to install the Test Player software.

Step 2
Create a test/study guide, and then use the Online Test Wizard to set up the online (LAN-based) test. Save your work and exit the *ExamView* software.

Step 3
Transfer the test/study guide file [e.g., chapter1.tst (Windows) or Chapter 1 (Macintosh)] and any accompanying multimedia files from your computer to the local area network server.

Copy the files from your hard drive to the folder set up by your network administrator. You need only copy the test file unless you linked an audio or video segment to one or more questions.

Step 4
Instruct your students to complete the test/study guide.

Students must have access to a computer connected to the local area network on which the Test Player and test/study guide are stored.

Step 5
After all students finish taking the test, copy the test/study guide file back to your hard drive. It is recommended that you copy the test to a different location from the original test file. The test file, itself, contains all of the students' results.

Note: If you set up a class roster, the test file will contain item analysis information and the results for each student. If you did not set up a roster, no results are recorded so you do not have to complete this step or the next.

Step 6
Start the *ExamView* software and open the test file to view your students' results.

CREATING AN ONLINE (LAN-BASED) TEST

Follow the steps shown below to create an online (LAN-based) test or study guide. Depending on the options you set, you can create a test or study guide. Before you begin, make sure that you installed the *ExamView* test generator and test player software. **Note**: See the next section (page 12) for instructions to set up the test player. (See page 15 for Internet testing features.)

Step 1
Start the *ExamView* software.

Step 2
Create or open a test/study guide.

Select the questions you want to include on the test. You can include any of the following types: True/False, Multiple Choice, Yes/No, Numeric Response, Completion, and Matching.

Step 3
Select the *Online Test Wizard* option from the **Online** menu.

ExamView presents step-by-step instructions to help you prepare the online test/study guide. (See Figure 4.) Read the instructions provided and complete each step. **Note**: Click the **Help** button if you need more assistance.

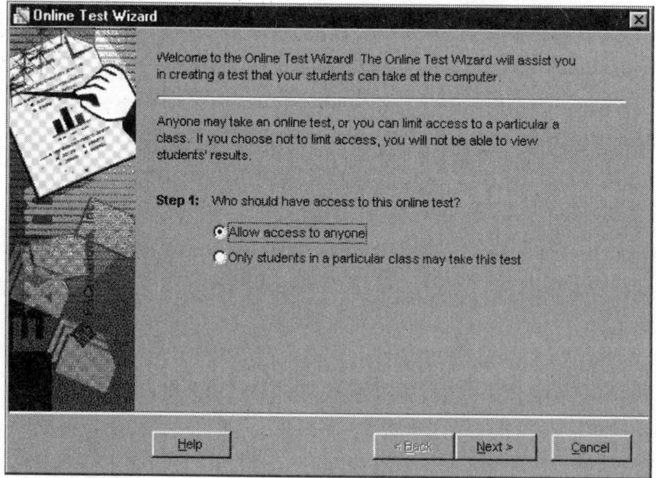

Figure 4 – Online Test Wizard (Step 1)

Step 4
Click the **Finish** button after you complete the last step using the Online Test Wizard. As you can see in Figure 5 on page 11, *ExamView* shows a summary that describes the settings for the online test.

Step 5
Save the test/study guide to a location where your students can easily access it. For example, save it in the same location where you installed the Test Player program.

It is recommended that you save the test/study guide to a location on a network server where students have read/write access. The Test Player will store all of your students' results (if you entered a class roster) in the test file itself. You can copy the test to individual computers, but this configuration takes more time to gather the results.

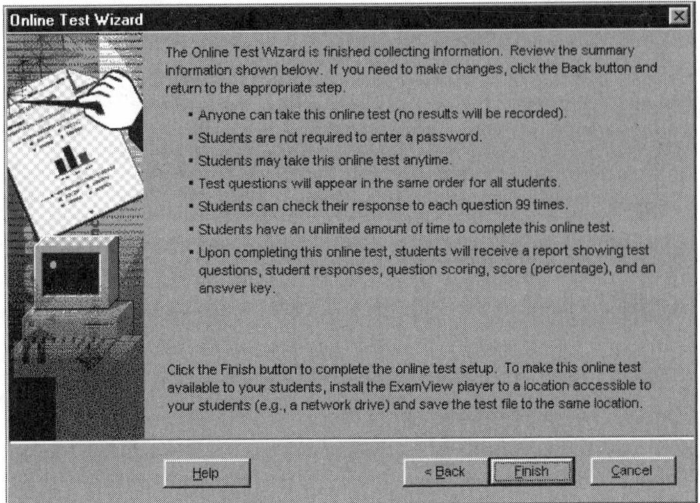

Figure 5 – Online Test Wizard (Summary)

Step 6
If you included multimedia links in any of the questions, copy those files to the same location where you saved the test/study guide.

If the multimedia files are on a CD-ROM or DVD disc, you may leave them on the disc, but provide this information to your students. To play one of these links, students will have to specify the location of the multimedia file.

NOTES:
- Use the *Test Preferences* and *Class Roster* options in the **Online** menu if you want to make any changes to the test parameters. These two options let you change any of the settings you selected using the Online Test Wizard.
- You must close the test before your students can access it with the Test Player.
- If you set up a class roster for a test/study guide, you cannot modify the test (e.g., edit a question, change the order, etc.) once any student has taken it unless you clear the results first.
- Provide your students with the Test Player setup program and a copy of the test/study guide if you want them to take it at home.

INSTALLING THE TEST PLAYER

Follow the instructions provided here to install the Test Player program for your students. You may copy the Test Player to a network (recommended), install it on individual computers, or provide it on floppy disk for your students to take home.

Even if you have a network, you can install the Test Player on individual computers. Students will still be able to access tests/study guides you store on a local area network.

ExamView Test Player Installation

Windows

Step 1
Turn on your computer.

Step 2
Insert the *ExamView* disc into your CD-ROM drive. If the software was provided on floppy disks, insert the *ExamView–Test Player* installation disk into Drive A.

Step 3
Click the **Start** button on the *Taskbar* and choose the *Run* option.

Step 4
If the *ExamView* software is provided on a CD-ROM, use the drive letter that corresponds to the CD-ROM drive on your computer (e.g., **d:\evplayer\setup** or **d:\evpro\evplayer\setup**).

If you are installing the software from a floppy disk, type **a:\setup** and press **Enter** to run the installation program.

Step 5
When prompted for a location to install the program, select a folder (e.g., **x:\programs\evplayer** for network installations or **c:\evplayer** on your local hard drive).

Step 6
For local area network (LAN) installations, complete the following steps at each workstation:

- Click the **Start** button and choose **Taskbar** from the **Settings** menu.
- Click the **Start Menu Programs** tab and click **Add.**
- Type the location and program name for the Test Player software, or use the **Browse** button to enter this information (e.g., **x:\programs\evplayer\evplayer.exe**).
- Proceed to the next screen and add a new folder (e.g., **ExamView Test Player**).
- Enter **ExamView Test Player** as the shortcut name and then click the **Finish** button.

Repeat Steps 1–5 if you plan to install the software at each computer instead of installing the program once on your network.

Macintosh

Step 1
Turn on your computer.

Step 2
Insert the *ExamView* installation disc into your CD-ROM drive. If the program is provided on floppy disks, insert the *ExamView–Test Player* installation disk into a disk drive.

Step 3
Open the installer window, if necessary.

Step 4
Double-click the installation icon to start the program.

Note: The installation program is configured to copy the test player to a new folder on your hard drive. You can, however, change this location. For example, you can select a location on your network server.

Step 5
When prompted for a location to install the program, select a folder on your local area network that is accessible to all students. If you are installing the software on a stand-alone computer, choose a location on the hard drive.

Step 6
At each workstation, enable file sharing and program linking if you installed the application on your network server.

For stand-alone computers, repeat Steps 1–5.

Installing the Test Player at Home

You can give your students the Test Player software to take home. If the *ExamView* software was sent to you on floppy disks, give your students the separate Test Player setup disk. If you received the software on CD-ROM, copy all of the setup files in the ***evplayer*** folder onto a floppy disk. Students should follow Steps 1-5 to install the software on their computer. When students take a test home, they should copy it into the same folder as the Test Player program.

TAKING AN ONLINE (LAN-BASED) TEST

Make sure that you have properly installed the *ExamView* Test Player software and copied the test/study guide to a location easily accessible to your students. If you linked multimedia files to any of the questions, it is recommended that you copy those files to the same folder as the test/study guide.

If you created a test with a class roster, students must correctly enter their IDs to be able to take the test/study guide. Provide this information to your students, if necessary. **Note**: If you do not want to track student scores, you should set up a test to allow anyone to take it.

Step 1
Start the *ExamView* Test Player software.

Step 2
Enter your name and ID. (See Figure 6.)

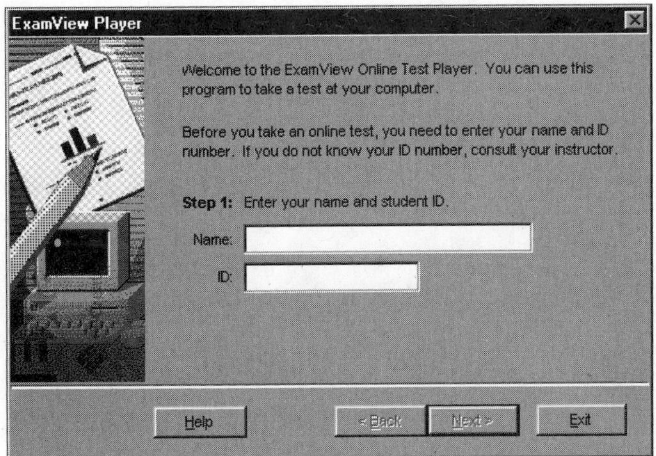

Figure 6 – Online Test/Study Guide Registration

Step 3
Select a test/study guide. (See Figure 7.)

If no tests (or study guides) appear in the list, click the **Folder** button to identify where the tests are located.

Step 4
(Optional) Enter a password, if prompted.

Step 5
Review the summary information and click **Start** when you are ready to begin.

Step 6
Answer all of the questions and click the **End** button when you finish.

Verify that you want to end the test. If you do not answer all of the questions in one session, you will ***not*** be able to resume the test at a later time.

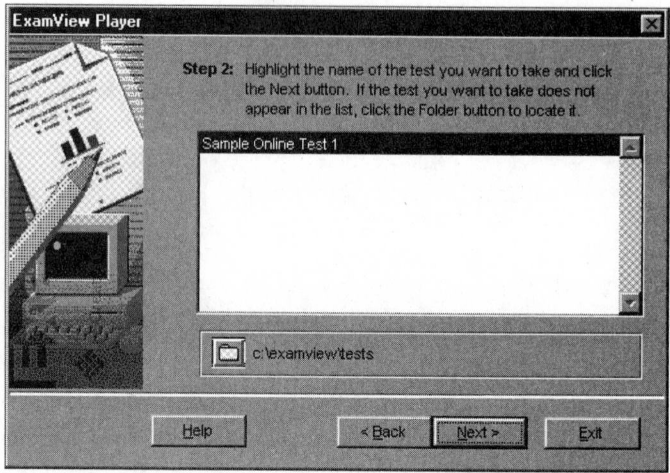

Figure 7 – Online Test/Study Guide Selection

Step 7
Review the test report.

Step 8
Click **New Test** to take another test or click **Exit** to quit the program.

VIEWING ONLINE (LAN-BASED) RESULTS

If you set up a test with a class roster (instead of allowing anyone to access a test/study guide), the *ExamView* Test Player will automatically collect the results for each student. The program saves this information in the test/study guide file itself.

Step 1
Start the *ExamView* software and open the online test/study guide that your students have already taken.

Step 2
Choose *View Test Results* from the **Online** menu.

Step 3
Review the results, item-by-item analysis, and statistics reports.

Step 4
Choose *Export Test Results* if you want to export the scores to your favorite gradebook program or spreadsheet application.

SECTION 4 — INTERNET TESTING

ExamView lets you easily create Internet tests and study guides. Build a test and then simply choose the *Publish Internet Test* option. You can choose to post tests to your own website or to publish tests directly to the *ExamView* website. (Visit us at www.examview.com to learn more about subscribing to the Internet test-hosting service.)

With the Internet test-hosting feature, you can publish a test or study guide directly to the *ExamView* website. Simply create a test and then follow the easy step-by-step instructions to publish it to the Internet. It's that simple! You can manage tests online, view reports, and download results. Students access your tests from one convenient location.

If you do not use the ExamView test-hosting service, you can manually post tests/study guides to your own website. If you create a test, your students' results are sent to you via email automatically. Or, you can create a study guide that your students can use to review various topics at their own pace.

INTERNET TESTING FAQs

Review the FAQs (frequently asked questions) below for more information on the Internet test-hosting features available to *ExamView Pro 3.0* users.

What are the advantages to using the Internet test-hosting feature? (1) Publishing an Internet test to your own website and setting up links can be quite challenging. With the Internet test-hosting feature, the process is completely automated. In minutes, you can post a test to the Internet. (2) When you post tests/study guides to your own website, only a few options are available. Using the *ExamView* test-hosting service, you have many more options available such as setting up a class roster and viewing detailed item analysis reports.

How do you register for the test-hosting service? Visit our website at www.examview.com to learn how to register. Before you can post tests/study guides, you must sign up to obtain a valid instructor ID and a password.

Is there an additional charge for the Internet test-hosting service? Yes, there is an additional yearly subscription charge to use this service. If you received the *ExamView* software from a publisher, you may be eligible for a discount or a free trial membership. (See our website for current prices and special promotions.)

Do you have to use the Internet test-hosting service? No, using the test-hosting service is not required. The *Publish Internet Test* feature includes an option to save an Internet test/study guide to a local hard drive. Then, you can manually post it to your own website.

Why aren't the same features available for tests posted to my own website? To offer the numerous Internet test-hosting features, we have developed many programs and databases that are stored on our servers. If you post to your own server or website, these programs are not available.

IMPORTANT: Your students must use a browser such as Netscape 4.0/Internet Explorer 4.0 (or a more recent version) that supports cascading style sheets (CSS1) and JavaScript. To post tests or study guides for delivery via the Internet, you must have your own access to an Internet server.

USING THE INTERNET TEST-HOSTING SERVICE

Using the *ExamView* test generator software, you can publish tests directly to the *ExamView* website if you have signed up for the test-hosting service. With a few simple steps, you can publish tests and study guides directly to the Internet. Refer to the following instructions to register for the Internet test-hosting service, create a test, publish a test to the Internet, take tests online, manage tests, and view student results.

Register for the Internet Test-Hosting Service

Step 1

Launch your web browser and go to www.examview.com.

Step 2

Go to the **Instructor Center** to register for the test-hosting service. Follow the instructions provided at the website to sign up.

Record the instructor ID and password assigned to you. You will need this information to publish a test or study guide to the *ExamView* website. When you choose to publish a test, you will be prompted to enter this information.

Step 3

Quit the browser.

Publish a Test/Study Guide to the ExamView Website

Step 1

Start the *ExamView* software.

Step 2

Create a new test or open an existing test.

Select the questions you want to include on the test. You can include any of the twelve (12) question types on a test, but only the objective questions are scored.

Step 3

Select the *Publish Internet Test* option from the **File** menu.

ExamView presents a window with various Internet testing options to help you prepare the online test. (See Figure 8.) **Note**: Click the **Help** button if you need more assistance.

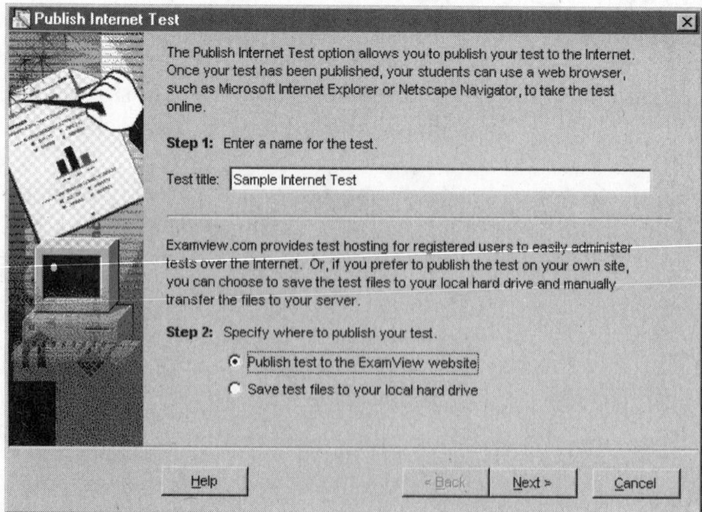

Figure 8 – Publish Internet Test Window

Step 4
Name the test.

Step 5
Select the option to publish your test to the *ExamView* website, and then click the **Next** button.

Step 6
Enter your instructor ID and password.

If you do not already have an instructor ID and password, click the **Register Now** button to launch your web browser and go to the www.examview.com website. You cannot proceed until you have a valid instructor ID and password.

Step 7
Choose whether you want to publish a test or a study guide.

Step 8
Specify when students may access the test/study guide.

Step 9
Enter the expiration date.

Step 10
Specify who should have access to this test/study guide.

Anyone may take it, or you may limit access to a particular group of students. If you specify a roster, students must enter an ID and password.

Step 11
Enter a student password, and click **Next**.

Step 12
Review the summary information. Click the **Back** button if you need to make changes. (See Figure 9.)

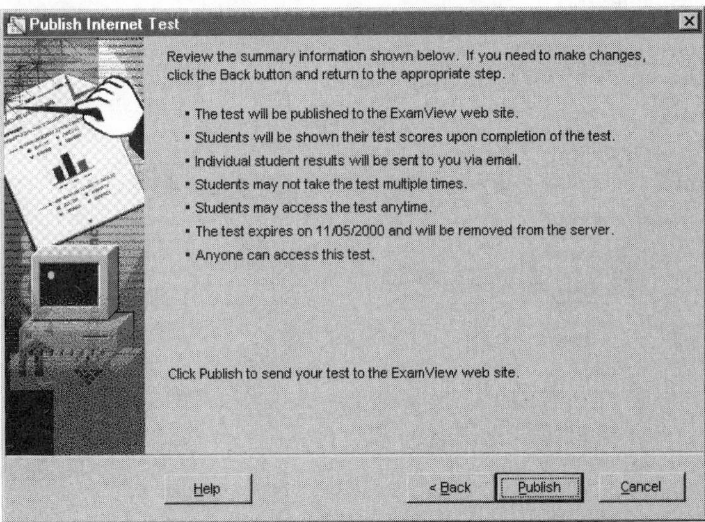

Figure 9 – Publish Internet Test Window (Summary)

Step 13

Click the **Publish** button when you are ready to post the test/study guide to the *ExamView* website.

The program automatically connects to the Internet and posts the test/study guide to the *ExamView* server. Access the instructor options on the *ExamView* website (www.examview.com) to preview a test, change selected parameters, or view results. If you need to edit or delete questions, you must change the test locally and then publish a new version. **Note:** An Internet connection is required to publish a test/study guide.

Step 14

Print a copy of the test/study guide for your records, create another test, or exit the software if you are finished.

Take a Test/Study Guide Online at www.evtestcenter.com

Once you publish a test/study guide to the *ExamView* server, anyone in the world can access it if you provide him or her with your instructor ID and the appropriate password. (**IMPORTANT:** ***Do not*** *give students your password, just your ID.*) Provide the instructions below to your students so that they can take the test or study guide.

Note: You must use a browser such as Netscape 4.0/Internet Explorer 4.0 (or a more recent version) that supports cascading style sheets level 1 (CSS1) and JavaScript. An active Internet connection is also required.

To take a test:

Step 1

Start your web browser.

Step 2

Go to the URL: www.evtestcenter.com.

Step 3

Enter your instructor's ID code. (See Figure 10.)

Upon entering a valid instructor code, you will see a list of tests your instructor has published.

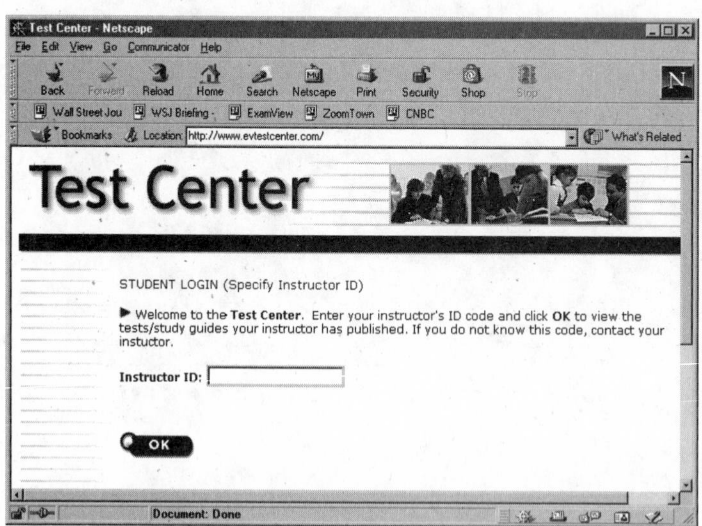

Figure 10 – Test Center Login (www.evtestcenter.com)

Step 4

Select a test.

Step 5
Enter your name (if requested), student ID, and student password.

Contact your instructor if you have not been assigned a student ID or you do not have a student password.

Step 6
Review the test and respond to all of the questions. (See the sample test in Figure 11.)

If you need help while working with a test, click the **Help** button shown at the bottom of the test. Click the browser's **Back** button to return to the test.

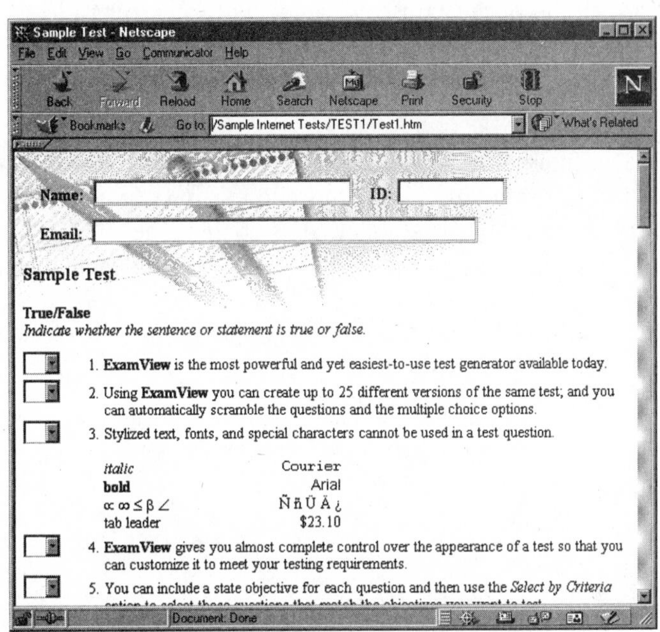

Figure 11 – Sample Internet Test

Step 7
When you complete the test, review the entire test and then click the **Grade & Submit** button located at the bottom of the test.

Your results will be emailed to your instructor. Depending on the test settings, you may be notified of your results immediately.

To complete a study guide:

Step 1
Start your web browser.

Step 2
Go to the URL: www.evtestcenter.com.

Step 3
Enter your instructor's ID.

You will see a list of study guides and tests your instructor has published.

Step 4
Select a study guide.

Step 5
Enter your name (if requested), student ID, and password.

Contact your instructor if you have not been assigned a student ID or you do not have a password.

Step 6
Review the study guide and answer all of the questions.

If you need help while working with a study guide, click the **Help** button shown at the bottom of the screen. Click the browser's **Back** button to return to the study guide.

Step 7
When you complete the study guide, review your responses and then click the **Check Your Work** button located at the bottom of the study guide.

Your work is scored and you will see whether you answered each question correctly or incorrectly. No results are sent to your instructor.

Step 8
Click the **Reset** button to erase all of your responses if you want to start over.

Review Student Results and Manage Tests

When your students complete an Internet test, their results are automatically stored on the server so that you can easily access this information. If you chose to receive results via email, you will also receive the following information for each student: (1) student name and ID, (2) raw score and percentage score for objective-based questions, and (3) responses for each question (objective and open-ended questions).

At the *ExamView* website, you may also change test-setup options, preview tests, download student results, and view your account information.

Step 1
Start your web browser.

Step 2
Go to the URL: www.examview.com and access the Instructor Center.

Step 3
Log in using your instructor ID and password to view the main menu options. (See Figure 12.)

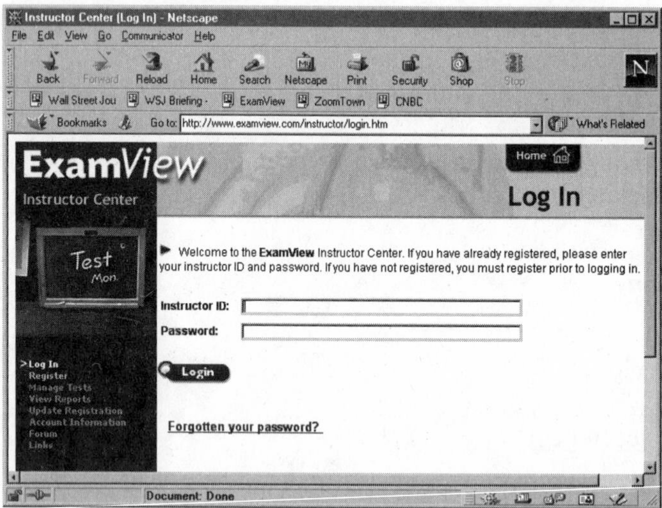

Figure 12 – *ExamView* Website (Instructor Center)

PUBLISHING TESTS TO YOUR OWN WEBSITE

If you choose not to sign up for the *ExamView* test-hosting service, you can still publish tests/study guides to your own website. You must save the test/study guide to your hard drive, upload the files to your website, and then provide access to your students. Refer to the following sections for step-by-step instructions.

Save an Internet Test/Study Guide to Your Hard Drive

Follow the steps shown below to create an Internet test/study guide and save it to your hard drive. Before you begin, make sure that you installed the *ExamView* test generator software.

Step 1
Start the *ExamView* software.

Step 2
Create a new test or open an existing test.

Select the questions you want to include on the test. You can include any of the twelve (12) question types on a test, but only the objective questions will be graded.

Step 3
Select the *Publish Internet Test* option from the **File** menu.

ExamView presents a window with various Internet testing options to help you prepare the online test. (See Figure 13.) **Note**: Click the **Help** button if you need more assistance.

Step 4
Name the test.

Step 5
Select the option to save the test files to your local hard drive, and then click the **Next** button.

Step 6
Choose whether you want to publish a test or a study guide.

Step 7
Review the summary information. Make changes, if necessary.

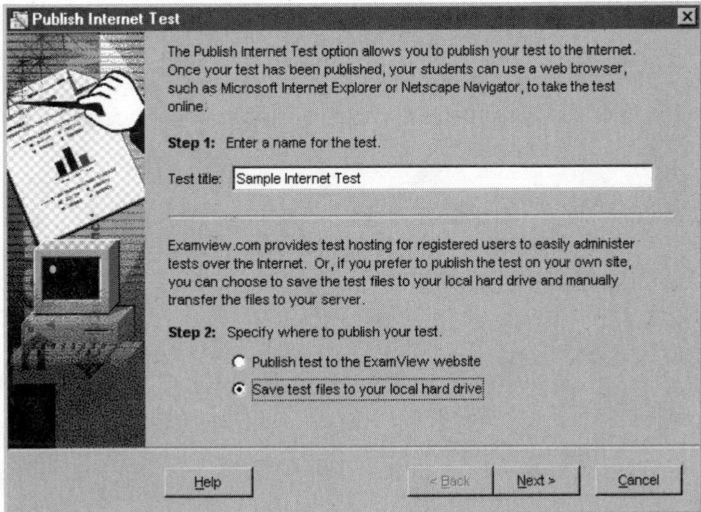

Figure 13 – Publish Internet Test Window

Step 8
Click the **Save** button to save the test/study guide files.

When you choose to save an Internet test to your local hard drive, *ExamView* creates an HTML file and an accompanying folder with all of the necessary image files. This makes it easier for you to post the files to a web server. If, for example, you enter a path such as **c:\examview\tests\chapter1** (Windows) or **HD:ExamView:Tests:Chapter1** (Macintosh), the software will create a file called **chapter1.htm** and a new folder called **chapter1_files** with all of the required picture files. (See the illustration below.)

Step 9
Post the test/study guide to a server to make it available to your students. (See the next section for instructions for posting a test to a server.)

Step 10
Once you post a test, you should verify that students can access it. You may also want to try the "Grade & Submit" feature for tests to make sure that the results are emailed to the correct address.

Note: When you create a test, *ExamView* encrypts the answer information so that a student cannot see the answers in the HTML page source. While this does help to prevent cheating, there is no foolproof method in an unsupervised environment.

Post a Test to Your Own Internet/Intranet Server

Once you save a test/study guide formatted for the Internet, you must post all of the related files to a location on a server that your students can access. You can post the files to a local area network, Intranet server, or an Internet server. You ***must*** have an Internet connection for students to be able to submit test results. (This is not required for a study guide.)

Note: Posting to a server can be a complex process. The specific steps will vary depending on the hardware and software configuration of your server. If you are not familiar with the required steps, contact your network administrator for assistance.

Step 1
Start an FTP program or other utility that allows you to copy files from your hard drive to an Internet/Intranet server.

Step 2
Log in to your server.

Step 3
Create a new folder on your server to hold the test/study guide files.

Step 4
Copy the **HTML** file and the accompanying folder to a location on your server that your students can access.

When you choose to save an Internet test to your hard drive, *ExamView* creates an HTML file and an accompanying folder with all of the necessary image files. This makes it easier for you to post the files to a web server.

IMPORTANT: By default, all of the file names are lowercase. Do not change the case since these files are referenced in the HTML document. You ***must*** copy the HTML file and the accompanying folder as is. Do not copy the HTML file into the corresponding folder. (See the illustration below.)

Step 5
Log off the server, if necessary.

Step 6
Record the URL for the test/study guide HTML document or set up a link to the test.

Take a Test or Study Guide Using the Internet

Once you post a test on a server, anyone in the world can access the test if you provide him or her with the Web (URL) address. Follow the instructions provided below to take a test or study guide.

Note: You must use a browser such as Netscape 4.0/Internet Explorer 4.0 (or a more recent version) that supports cascading style sheets level 1 (CSS1) and JavaScript. An active Internet connection is required to submit test results.

To take a test via the Internet:

Step 1
Start your web browser.

Step 2
Type the web address (URL) and test name (e.g., **www.school.edu/economics/test1.htm**), or enter an address for a page with a link to the test. (See the sample test in Figure 14.)

If the test is located on a local area network, use the open page command in the browser to open the test.

Step 3
Enter your name, student ID, and email address (optional).

Step 4
Answer all of the questions.

If you need help while working with a test, click the **Help** button shown at the bottom of the test. Click the browser's **Back** button to return to the test.

Step 5
When you complete the test, review your responses and then click the **Grade & Submit** button located at the bottom of the screen.

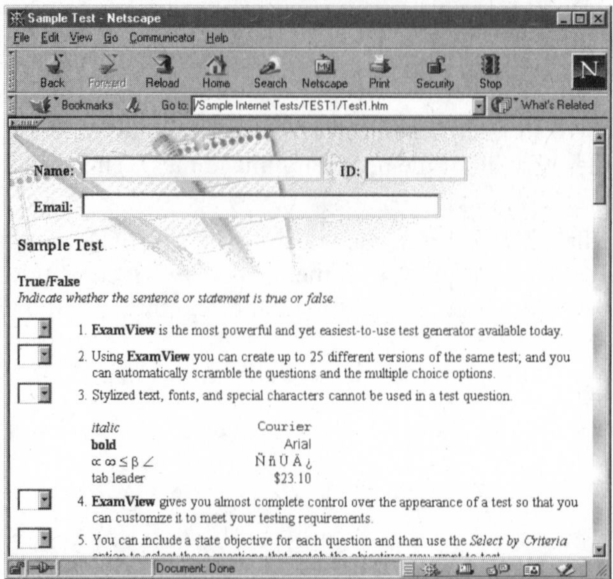

Figure 14 – Sample Internet Test

To complete a study guide via the Internet:

Step 1

Start your web browser.

Step 2

Type the web address (URL) and study guide name (e.g., **www.school.edu/history/study.htm**), or enter an address for a page with a link to the study guide.

Step 3

Enter your name.

Step 4

Answer all of the questions.

Step 5

When you complete the study guide, review the entire test and then click the **Check Your Work** button located at the bottom of the study guide.

Your work is scored and you will see whether you answered each question correctly or incorrectly. No results are sent to your instructor.

Step 6

Click the **Reset** button to erase all of your responses if you want to start over.

Receive Student Results via Email

When your students complete an Internet test, the browser sends the students' test results and all of their responses directly to you via email. The email will include the following information:

- student name and ID
- raw score and percentage score for objective-based questions
- responses for each question (objective and open-ended questions)

Note: **You will not receive any student results for Internet study guides.**

The Question Bank for *PowerPoint 2002 Comprehensive* uses the State Objective field ("STO") to list the Activity Codes for the Microsoft Office User Specialist ("MOUS") Certification Program. See "Appendix F" in the *PowerPoint 2002 Comprehensive* text for a listing and correlation of all MOUS Activities. In the actual Question Bank, all MOUS Activities are listed after the heading "STO" and are prefaced by "MOUS."

Lesson 1: What Is PowerPoint?

True/False

1. The status bar displays informative messages, such as the number of the slide you are viewing.
ANS: T
OBJ: 1-2
STO: MOUS PP2002 1-1
2. The easiest way to close a presentation or PowerPoint is to click the appropriate Close button in the top right corner of the window.
ANS: T
OBJ: 1-8
STO: MOUS PP2002 1-1
3. To create a file folder, you must open the My Computer window.
ANS: F
OBJ: 1-6
STO: MOUS PP2002 7-3
4. When you finish keying in a text box, you double-click any word to deactivate the text box.
ANS: F
OBJ: 1-3
STO: MOUS PP2002 2-2
5. When working in the Open File dialog box, you use the Up One Level button to move up one level in the hierarchy of folders listed in the Look In box.
ANS: T
OBJ: 1-1
STO: MOUS PP2002 1-1
6. If you point to a button on a toolbar, a ScreenTip appears displaying the button's name.
ANS: T
OBJ: 1-2
STO: MOUS PP2002 1-1
7. To open a presentation that is stored on a hard drive or diskette, click the Open button on the Standard toolbar.
ANS: T
OBJ: 1-1
STO: MOUS PP2002 1-1
8. When you start PowerPoint, only one toolbar is displayed.
ANS: F
OBJ: 1-1
STO: MOUS PP2002 1-1
9. When working in the Open dialog box, the preview option is found on the Tools menu.
ANS: F
OBJ: 1-1
STO: MOUS PP2002 1-1
10. You can use the Start button on the Windows taskbar to start PowerPoint.
ANS: T
OBJ: 1-1
STO: MOUS PP2002 1-1
11. You can print handouts only in Slide Sorter view.
ANS: F
OBJ: 1-7
STO: MOUS PP2002 5-1
12. If you rename a file with the Save As command, the original file is automatically deleted.
ANS: F
OBJ: 1-6
STO: MOUS PP2002 7-3
13. Clicking the right mouse button during a presentation displays a shortcut menu.
ANS: T
OBJ: 1-5
STO: MOUS PP2002 7-2
14. The Outline tab displays all the presentation's slide titles, subtitles, and body text.
ANS: T
OBJ: 1-4
STO: MOUS PP2002 1-1
15. During a slide show, pressing [PgUp] moves you to the previous slide.
ANS: T
OBJ: 1-5
STO: MOUS PP2002 7-2
16. Slide shows always begin with the first slide in your presentation.
ANS: F
OBJ: 1-5
STO: MOUS PP2002 7-2
17. During a slide show, when you use the pen pointer to draw a circle around a word, that circle becomes a permanent part of your presentation.
ANS: F
OBJ: 1-5
STO: MOUS PP2002 7-2
18. Task panes appear and change automatically to make appropriate commands available.
ANS: T
OBJ: 1-4
STO: MOUS PP2002 1-1
19. While running a slide show, you can jump to a different slide by using the keyboard command [Ctrl]+[G].
ANS: F
OBJ: 1-5
STO: MOUS PP2002 7-2
20. You can double-click a word in a text box to select it.
ANS: T
OBJ: 1-3
STO: MOUS PP2002 2-2

Multiple Choice

1. To start PowerPoint, you can use:
a. The Microsoft Office Shortcut bar
b. The PowerPoint shortcut icon
c. Windows Explorer
d. All of the above
ANS: d
OBJ: 1-1
STO: MOUS PP2002 1-1
2. The filename of a presentation file appears in the:
a. Status bar
b. Standard toolbar
c. Title bar

d. Task pane
ANS: c
OBJ: 1-6
STO: MOUS PP2002 7-3

3. To move through slides when running a slide show, you can use:
   a. The left mouse button to move forward and the right mouse button to move backward
   b. Any of the arrow keys
   c. [PgUp] or [PgDn] keys
   d. All of the above
   ANS: b
   OBJ: 1-5
   STO: MOUS PP2002 7-2

4. The [Ctrl]+[Home] and [Ctrl]+[End] keyboard commands move to the first or last slide in a presentation except in:
   a. Slide Sorter view
   b. Slide Show view
   c. The Slides pane
   d. The Outline pane
   ANS: b
   OBJ: 1-5
   STO: MOUS PP2002 7-2

5. The following are allowed when you name files:
   a. Spaces
   b. Asterisks
   c. Question marks
   d. All of the above
   ANS: a
   OBJ: 1-6
   STO: MOUS PP2002 7-3

6. To open a shortcut menu:
   a. Click the right mouse button
   b. Click the left mouse button
   c. Double-click the left mouse button
   d. Double-click the right mouse button
   ANS: a
   OBJ: 1-2
   STO: MOUS PP2002 1-1

7. In PowerPoint, as well as Windows, filenames are limited to:
   a. 300 characters
   b. 255 characters
   c. 10 characters
   d. 8 characters
   ANS: b
   OBJ: 1-6
   STO: MOUS PP2002 7-3

8. To close a PowerPoint presentation, you can:
   a. Click the Close Window button
   b. Choose Close from the File menu
   c. Press [Ctrl]+[W]
   d. All of the above
   ANS: d
   OBJ: 1-8
   STO: MOUS PP2002 1-1

9. A floating toolbar:
   a. Can be displayed only when the task pane is closed
   b. Can be moved to any location on your screen
   c. Makes it easy to run a slide show
   d. All of the above
   ANS: b
   OBJ: 1-2
   STO: MOUS PP2002 1-1

10. To close PowerPoint, you can:
   a. Right-click the Windows Start button
   b. Choose Exit from the File menu
   c. Press [Alt]+[F5]
   d. All of the above
   ANS: b
   OBJ: 1-8
   STO: MOUS PP2002 1-1

11. The following are true of PowerPoint's Help features:
   a. You can key search words in the Ask a Question box
   b. You can click the Help button on the Standard toolbar
   c. You can use the Office Assistant
   d. All of the above
   ANS: d
   OBJ: 1-2
   STO: MOUS PP2002 1-1

12. Using the Save As command gives an existing presentation:
   a. A new filename
   b. The same filename
   c. The same filename in the Favorites directory
   d. None of the above
   ANS: a
   OBJ: 1-6
   STO: MOUS PP2002 7-3

13. The Save command or button:
   a. Always makes the Save As dialog box appear
   b. Saves all changes in a new file, keeping the original file as it was before making changes
   c. Saves all changes you made to the presentation since you last opened or saved it
   d. All of the above
   ANS: c
   OBJ: 1-6
   STO: MOUS PP2002 7-3

14. When you are keying text, the following keys work the same way they do when you use a word processor:
   a. [Backspace]
   b. [Delete]
   c. [Enter]
   d. All of the above
   ANS: d
   OBJ: 1-3
   STO: MOUS PP2002 2-2

15. To print a presentation:
   a. Choose Print from the Edit menu
   b. Press [Shift]+[P]
   c. Click the Print button
   d. All of the above
   ANS: c
   OBJ: 1-7
   STO: MOUS PP2002 5-1

16. During a slide show, to change an arrow pointer to a pen:
   a. Press [Ctrl]+[P]
   b. Choose Pointer Options from the Shortcut menu
   c. a or b
   d. Press [Ctrl]+[Right Arrow]
   ANS: c
   OBJ: 1-5
   STO: MOUS PP2002 7-4

17. During a slide show, you can choose from a list of slide titles by:
   a. Choosing Meeting Minder from the shortcut menu
   b. Choosing Go from the shortcut menu
   c. Pressing [Ctrl]+[N]
   d. None of the above
   ANS: b

OBJ: 1-5
STO: MOUS PP2002 7-2

18. To see a preview of slides or handouts before printing them:
    a. Run a slide show after setting print options
    b. From the View menu choose Preview
    c. Click the Preview button on the Print dialog box
    d. Click the Print View button in the lower-left corner of the screen

    ANS: c
    OBJ: 1-7
    STO: MOUS PP2002 5-1
19. To print a presentation as audience handouts:
    a. Choose Handouts in the Print dialog box
    b. Double-click the Print button in any view
    c. Change to Slide Sorter view and then press the Print button
    d. All of the above

    ANS: a
    OBJ: 1-7
    STO: MOUS PP2002 5-1
20. To start a slide show on the fifth slide of your presentation:
    a. In Outline view, click the slide 5 icon and then click the Slide Show button
    b. In Slide Sorter view, select slide 5 and then click the Slide Show button
    c. In Slide view, move to slide 5 and then click the Slide Show button
    d. All of the above

    ANS: d
    OBJ: 1-5
    STO: MOUS PP2002 7-2

Completion

1. If you want to dock a floating toolbar, double-click ____________.
   ANS: Its title bar
   OBJ: 1-2
   STO: MOUS PP2002 1-1
2. If you allow your mouse pointer to rest on a toolbar button, a ____________ appears.
   ANS: ScreenTip
   OBJ: 1-2
   STO: MOUS PP2002 1-1
3. Clicking the ____________ button sends a presentation directly to the printer using previously defined settings.
   ANS: Print
   OBJ: 1-7
   STO: MOUS PP2002 5-1
4. To open an existing presentation, click the Open button on the ____________ toolbar.
   ANS: Standard
   OBJ: 1-1
   STO: MOUS PP2002 1-1
5. You use ____________ bars to move the screen's display right or left and up or down within a slide.
   ANS: Scroll
   OBJ: 1-2
   STO: MOUS PP2002 1-1
6. A dotted box that contains sample text you replace is called a ____________.
   ANS: Placeholder
   OBJ: 1-3
   STO: MOUS PP2002 2-2
7. To open an existing presentation, you can choose ____________ from the File menu.
   ANS: Open
   OBJ: 1-1
   STO: MOUS PP2002 1-1
8. A wavy red underline beneath a word indicates ____________.
   ANS: A spelling (or other) error
   OBJ: 1-3
   STO: MOUS PP2002 2-2
9. The fastest way to close a presentation or PowerPoint program is to click the appropriate ____________ button.
   ANS: Close
   OBJ: 1-8
   STO: MOUS PP2002 1-1
10. When you edit text in the Outline tab, the changes are also seen in the ____________ pane.
    ANS: Slide
    OBJ: 1-4
    STO: MOUS PP2002 1-1
11. To save a document, you can use the keyboard combination ____________.
    ANS: [Ctrl]+[S]
    OBJ: 1-6
    STO: MOUS PP2002 7-3
12. When running a slide show, press ____________ to view the next slide.
    ANS: [PgDn] or [Down Arrow] or [Right Arrow] or [N]
    OBJ: 1-5
    STO: MOUS PP2002 7-2
13. When using the Open dialog box to open a file in another folder, you can click the down arrow to the right of the ____________ drop-down list.
    ANS: Look In
    OBJ: 1-1
    STO: MOUS PP2002 1-1
14. Certain submenus can be floated by ____________.
    ANS: Dragging the bar at the top of the menu
    OBJ: 1-2
    STO: MOUS PP2002 1-1
15. When you print audience handouts, the maximum number of slides per page is ____________.
    ANS: Nine
    OBJ: 1-7
    STO: MOUS PP2002 5-1
16. To make a slide show begin on slide 3, before clicking the Slide Show button, you must first ____________.
    ANS: Select (or display) slide 3
    OBJ: 1-5
    STO: MOUS PP2002 7-3
17. If the Outline and Slides pane is not showing, click the ____________ button to display it.
    ANS: Normal View
    OBJ: 1-4
    STO: MOUS PP2002 1-1
18. When running a slide show, you can find Pointer Options on the ____________ menu.
    ANS: Shortcut
    OBJ: 1-5
    STO: MOUS PP2002 7-2
19. A small dot placed to the left of each item in a list is called a ____________.
    ANS: Bullet
    OBJ: 1-3
    STO: MOUS PP2002 2-2

20. You can remove a circle that you drew on a slide during a slide show by choosing ________________ from the shortcut menu.
ANS: Screen, Erase Pen
OBJ: 1-5
STO: MOUS PP2002 7-2

Lesson 2: Basic Presentation Skills

True/False

1. When you use the AutoContent Wizard dialog box to create a presentation, a green square indicates which step of the process you are currently working on.
ANS: T
OBJ: 2-1
STO: MOUS PP2002 1-1

2. To select an entire sentence in a placeholder, press [Ctrl] and click the left mouse button on any word in that sentence.
ANS: T
OBJ: 2-1
STO: MOUS PP2002 2-2

3. To select a word quickly in a placeholder, single-click the mouse on that word.
ANS: F
OBJ: 2-1
STO: MOUS PP2002 2-2

4. You can move the Spelling dialog box out of the way by dragging its title bar.
ANS: T
OBJ: 2-3
STO: MOUS PP2002 2-2

5. You can add your own custom AutoCorrect entries to correct common typos or to expand abbreviations.
ANS: T
OBJ: 2-3
STO: MOUS PP2002 2-2

6. The Collate option on the Print dialog box can be selected when you print multiple copies.
ANS: T
OBJ: 2-7
STO: MOUS PP2002 5-1

7. An animation scheme must be applied individually to each slide in a presentation.
ANS: F
OBJ: 2-5
STO: MOUS PP2002 4-3

8. You can turn AutoCorrect on or off by using the Customize command on the Tools menu.
ANS: F
OBJ: 2-3
STO: MOUS PP2002 2-2

9. When using the style checker, you should check to see if PowerPoint changed any proper nouns, such as names or days of the week, to lowercase.
ANS: T
OBJ: 2-3
STO: MOUS PP2002 2-2

10. Misspelled words in a presentation are flagged by a green wavy line.
ANS: F
OBJ: 2-3
STO: MOUS PP2002 2-2

11. From the Headers and Footers dialog box, you can choose to display a date on slides or notes and handouts that either remains fixed or updates automatically.
ANS: T
OBJ: 2-6
STO: MOUS PP2002 1-3

12. To print slides 1 through 5, you key 1:5 in the Print dialog box.
ANS: F
OBJ: 2-7
STO: MOUS PP2002 5-1

13. To print multiple, nonconsecutive slides such as slides 1, 4, and 6, you key 1,4,6 in the Print dialog box.
ANS: T
OBJ: 2-7
STO: MOUS PP2002 5-1

14. You can use the Find Whole Words Only option in the Find dialog box to prevent words that are embedded in larger words from being found.
ANS: T
OBJ: 2-4
STO: MOUS PP2002 2-2

15. You must hold down the [Alt] key while dragging to move a slide to a new position in Slide Sorter view.
ANS: F
OBJ: 2-2
STO: MOUS PP2002 4-8

16. If the Office Assistant pops up, you can turn it off permanently by right-clicking it and choosing Hide.
ANS: F
OBJ: 2-3
STO: MOUS PP2002 2-2

17. Pressing [Alt]+[Right Arrow] moves the insertion point to the beginning of the next word.
ANS: F
OBJ: 2-1
STO: MOUS PP2002 2-2

18. The Header and Footer command is found in the Insert menu.
ANS: F
OBJ: 2-6
STO: MOUS PP2002 1-3

19. If PowerPoint is already open, you can use the AutoContent Wizard to create a new presentation by clicking the New button on the Standard toolbar.
ANS: F
OBJ: 2-1
STO: MOUS PP2002 2-2

20. You must be in Slide Sorter view or Outline view to delete a slide.
ANS: F
OBJ: 2-2
STO: MOUS PP2002 1-2

Multiple Choice

1. To display the Outline and Slides tabs:
   a. Choose Outline and Slides pane from the View menu
   b. Click the Outline View button
   c. Click the Normal View button
   d. None of the above

   ANS: c
   OBJ: 2-2
   STO: MOUS PP2002 4-8

2. While you are keying text, AutoCorrect corrects words automatically after you:
   a. Click the AutoCorrect button
   b. Press [Spacebar]
   c. Press the [Left Arrow] key
   d. All of the above
   ANS: b
   OBJ: 2-3
   STO: MOUS PP2002 2-2

3. To prevent the spell-checker from flagging an error it finds, you must:
   a. Press the [Esc] key
   b. Click Ignore
   c. Click Change
   d. All of the above
   ANS: b
   OBJ: 2-3
   STO: MOUS PP2002 2-2

4. If you use the Replace command to replace all occurrences of "am" with "pm," which of the following will not happen:
   a. "8:00 a.m." remains "8:00 a.m."
   b. "8:00 am" changes to "8:00 pm"
   c. "American" changes to "pmerican"
   d. "8:00 AM" changes to "8:00 pm"
   ANS: a
   OBJ: 2-4
   STO: MOUS PP2002 2-2

5. To apply a slide transition, you can:
   a. Choose Slide Transition from the Insert menu
   b. Choose Custom Animation from the Slide Show menu
   c. Choose Slide Transition from the Other Task Panes list box
   d. All of the above
   ANS: c
   OBJ: 2-5
   STO: MOUS PP2002 4-3

6. To print handouts with 4 slides per page:
   a. Key 1-4 in the slides box on the Print dialog box
   b. Choose Handouts (4 slides per page) in the Preview window
   c. Choose Notes Pages from the Print What list box in the Print dialog box
   d. None of the above
   ANS: c
   OBJ: 2-7
   STO: MOUS PP2002 5-1

7. You can use the Header and Footer dialog box to:
   a. Insert a date at the top of each slide
   b. Apply footers to all slides except the title slide
   c. Automatically insert the presentation filename and path
   d. All of the above
   ANS: b
   OBJ: 2-6
   STO: MOUS PP2002 1-3

8. The Pure Black and White option:
   a. Converts all colors to black or white, eliminating shades of gray
   b. Prints only the black and white items on the screen
   c. Converts all colors to shades of gray
   d. None of the above
   ANS: a
   OBJ: 2-7
   STO: MOUS PP2002 5-1

9. To start the spell-checker:
   a. Choose Spelling from the Edit menu
   b. Click the Spelling button
   c. Press [Alt]+[F7]
   d. All of the above
   ANS: b
   OBJ: 2-3
   STO: MOUS PP2002 2-2

10. The following formats are correct for specifying a range of slides to print:
    a. 1:3, 5
    b. 1 - 4
    c. 2, 4:6
    d. None of the above
    ANS: b
    OBJ: 2-7
    STO: MOUS PP2002 5-1

11. When printing, you can choose:
    a. Slides, handouts (1, 2, 3, 4, 6, or 9 to a page), notes, or outlines
    b. More than one copy
    c. Individual, multiple, or the current slide(s)
    d. All of the above
    ANS: d
    OBJ: 2-7
    STO: MOUS PP2002 5-1

12. To open the Header and Footer dialog box:
    a. Choose Header and Footer from the View menu
    b. Click the Header/Footer button on the Standard toolbar
    c. Press [Ctrl]+[E]
    d. None of the above
    ANS: a
    OBJ: 2-6
    STO: MOUS PP2002 1-3

13. To start the AutoContent Wizard:
    a. Choose From AutoContent Wizard in the New Presentation task pane
    b. Choose New from the File menu, click the General tab, and then double-click the AutoContent Wizard icon
    c. Click the AutoContent Wizard button
    d. a and b
    ANS: a
    OBJ: 2-1
    STO: MOUS PP2002 2-2

14. To move a slide in the Slides tab, you can:
    a. Select a thumbnail and then use the arrow keys
    b. Select a thumbnail and then press [Ctrl]+[arrow] key
    c. Drag a slide thumbnail up or down
    d. All of the above
    ANS: c
    OBJ: 2-2
    STO: MOUS PP2002 4-8

15. When the Slide pane is active, you can delete a slide by:
    a. Pressing the [Delete] key on your keyboard
    b. Choosing Delete Slide from the Edit menu
    c. Clicking the Delete button on the Standard toolbar
    d. All of the above
    ANS: b
    OBJ: 2-2
    STO: MOUS PP2002 1-2

16. The AutoContent Wizard dialog box enables you to:
    a. Enter the titles for all the slides in your presentation
    b. Choose the presentation's template design
    c. Enter a title for the presentation
    d. Choose the numbering style for slide numbers
    ANS: c

OBJ: 2-1
STO: MOUS PP2002 1-1

17. Which option is not available on the Slide Transition task pane:
    a. Reverse
    b. Speed
    c. Sound
    d. Apply to All Slides
    ANS: a
    OBJ: 2-5
    STO: MOUS PP2002 4-3

18. Using the Find dialog box, you can find the word "The" (and no other words) only when it begins a sentence by:
    a. Choosing the Find Whole Words Only option
    b. Capitalizing the word "The" and choosing both the Match Case and the Find Whole Words Only options
    c. Capitalizing the word "The" and keying an [asterisk] before and after the word
    d. Capitalizing the word "The," keying a [space] before and after the word, and choosing the Match Case option
    ANS: b
    OBJ: 2-4
    STO: MOUS PP2002 2-2

19. To select three noncontiguous slide thumbnails, you can:
    a. Hold down [Shift] and click each of the thumbnails
    b. Hold down [Alt] and click each of the thumbnails
    c. Hold down [Ctrl] and click each of the thumbnails
    d. None of the above
    ANS: c
    OBJ: 2-2
    STO: MOUS PP2002 4-8

20. You can change the position of a slide in a presentation by:
    a. Keying a new slide number under the slide in Slide Sorter view
    b. Cutting a slide in Slide view, displaying the slide after which the cut slide will be placed, and then pasting the slide
    c. Holding the [Ctrl] key while dragging the slide to a new position in Slide Sorter view
    d. None of the above
    ANS: d
    OBJ: 2-2
    STO: MOUS PP2002 4-8

Completion

1. To select a paragraph, ________________-click it with your mouse.
   ANS: Triple
   OBJ: 2-1
   STO: MOUS PP2002 2-2

2. To open the Find dialog box, you can use the keyboard shortcut ________________.
   ANS: [Ctrl]+[F]
   OBJ: 2-4
   STO: MOUS PP2002 2-2

3. To delete slides 2 through 5, select slide 2, press ________________ and select slide 5, and then press [Delete].
   ANS: [Shift]
   OBJ: 2-2
   STO: MOUS PP2002 1-2

4. To select a word, ________________-click it.
   ANS: Double
   OBJ: 2-1
   STO: MOUS PP2002 2-2

5. If a word has a red wavy underline, you can ________________ to display a shortcut list of suggested corrections.
   ANS: Right-click it
   OBJ: 2-3
   STO: MOUS PP2002 2-2

6. To delete the character to the left of the insertion point, press ________________.
   ANS: [Backspace]
   OBJ: 2-1
   STO: MOUS PP2002 2-2

7. To check spelling, click the Spelling button on the ________________ toolbar.
   ANS: Standard
   OBJ: 2-3
   STO: MOUS PP2002 2-2

8. A lightbulb icon indicates a possible ________________ error whenever it appears.
   ANS: Style
   OBJ: 2-3
   STO: MOUS PP2002 2-2

9. To delete the character to the right of the insertion point, press ________________.
   ANS: [Delete]
   OBJ: 2-1
   STO: MOUS PP2002 2-2

10. To print just the slide that is displayed, choose ________________ in the Print dialog box.
    ANS: Current Slide
    OBJ: 2-7
    STO: MOUS PP2002 5-1

11. An online guide that leads you through the steps to complete a task is called a ________________.
    ANS: Wizard
    OBJ: 2-1
    STO: MOUS PP2002 2-2

12. To delete the word to the left of the insertion point, press ________________.
    ANS: [Ctrl]+[Backspace]
    OBJ: 2-1
    STO: MOUS PP2002 2-2

13. To print presentations on a black-and-white printer with no grayscale shading, choose the ________________ print option.
    ANS: Pure Black and White
    OBJ: 2-7
    STO: MOUS PP2002 5-1

14. To delete the word to the right of the insertion point, press ________________.
    ANS: [Ctrl]+[Delete]
    OBJ: 2-1
    STO: MOUS PP2002 2-2

15. The AutoContent Wizard creates a presentation with a series of slides containing sample text. You can change the sample text by ________________.
    ANS: Selecting it and then keying new text in its place
    OBJ: 2-1
    STO: MOUS PP2002 2-2

16. The wording of the sample text that appears on slides created with the AutoContent Wizard depends on the ________________ that you choose.

ANS: Presentation type
OBJ: 2-1
STO: MOUS PP2002 2-2

17. If you choose the Date and Time option for Notes and Handouts in the Header and Footer dialog box, the date will appear in the __________ corner of the page.
ANS: Upper-right
OBJ: 2-6
STO: MOUS PP2002 1-3

18. In Slide Sorter view, you can change the position of a slide by __________.
ANS: Dragging it to a new location
OBJ: 2-2
STO: MOUS PP2002 4-8

19. To open the Replace dialog box, you can use the keyboard shortcut __________.
ANS: [Ctrl]+[H]
OBJ: 2-4
STO: MOUS PP2002 2-2

20. You can see how your handouts will appear on paper in the __________ window.
ANS: Preview
OBJ: 2-7
STO: MOUS PP2002 5-1

Lesson 3: Creating a Presentation from Scratch

True/False

1. To start a new, blank presentation, you can click the New button on the Standard toolbar.
ANS: T
OBJ: 3-1
STO: MOUS PP2002 1-1

2. To move to the next placeholder, press [Enter].
ANS: F
OBJ: 3-1
STO: MOUS PP2002 1-1

3. You can click the Promote button to indent selected text to the right.
ANS: F
OBJ: 3-3
STO: MOUS PP2002 2-2

4. The Undo button can undo only your last action.
ANS: F
OBJ: 3-4
STO: MOUS PP2002 2-2

5. The Redo button reapplies editing commands in the order you undid them.
ANS: T
OBJ: 3-4
STO: MOUS PP2002 2-2

6. You can change layouts on slides by clicking the Slide Layout button on the Formatting toolbar.
ANS: T
OBJ: 3-7
STO: MOUS PP2002 1-2

7. If you copy a slide from one presentation to another, you will need to make color adjustments to make the copied slide match the new presentation.
ANS: F
OBJ: 3-2
STO: MOUS PP2002 1-2

8. You can display the Slide Design task pane by double-clicking the name of the current design appearing in the status bar.
ANS: T
OBJ: 3-5
STO: MOUS PP2002 1-1

9. You can change the color scheme for a single slide or for all slides in a presentation.
ANS: T
OBJ: 3-5
STO: MOUS PP2002 4-1

10. You can add notes for a slide by keying text in the Notes pane.
ANS: T
OBJ: 3-8
STO: MOUS PP2002 2-2

11. To promote a bulleted item, you can click the Decrease Indent button or press [Tab].
ANS: F
OBJ: 3-3
STO: MOUS PP2002 2-2

12. To add a new slide, press [Ctrl]+[M] or click New Slide on the Formatting toolbar.
ANS: T
OBJ: 3-2
STO: MOUS PP2002 1-2

13. To apply a design template, you can choose Slide Design from the Edit menu.
ANS: F
OBJ: 3-5
STO: MOUS PP2002 1-1

14. The Office Clipboard can store as many as 24 separate items, which can be pasted into your presentation when needed.
ANS: T
OBJ: 3-6
STO: MOUS PP2002 2-2

15. Only one presentation can be displayed on your screen at a time.
ANS: F
OBJ: 3-6
STO: MOUS PP2002 4-8

16. When you print speaker notes, you can choose specific slides for which to print the notes.
ANS: T
OBJ: 3-8
STO: MOUS PP2002 5-1

17. When a placeholder is activated, pressing [Esc] and then [Tab] selects a different object on the slide.
ANS: T
OBJ: 3-1
STO: MOUS PP2002 1-1

18. If you need to change a bulleted-list slide layout to a two-column layout, you must create a new slide with the proper layout and delete the old one.
ANS: F
OBJ: 3-7
STO: MOUS PP2002 4-4

19. If you press [Ctrl]+[M], a new slide is automatically inserted before the current slide.
ANS: F
OBJ: 3-2
STO: MOUS PP2002 1-2

20. If you click a second-level bullet, pressing [Shift]+[Tab] will promote it.
ANS: T
OBJ: 3-3
STO: MOUS PP2002 2-2

Multiple Choice

1. A slide layout can consist of:
   a. Body text and titles
   b. Tables
   c. Charts
   d. All of the above
   ANS: d
   OBJ: 3-7
   STO: MOUS PP2002 4-4
2. Which of the following actions will not create a new slide:
   a. Click New Slide on the Formatting toolbar
   b. Press [Ctrl]+[N]
   c. Choose New Slide from the Insert menu
   d. Press [Ctrl]+[Enter] one or more times
   ANS: b
   OBJ: 3-2
   STO: MOUS PP2002 1-2
3. To switch from one open presentation to another:
   a. Click the Tile button
   b. Click its name on the Windows taskbar
   c. Press [Ctrl]+[A]
   d. All of the above
   ANS: b
   OBJ: 3-6
   STO: MOUS PP2002 4-8
4. To open the Slide Layout dialog box:
   a. Choose Slide Layout from the Other Task Panes list box
   b. Choose Slide Layout from the Format menu
   c. Choose Slide Layout from the shortcut menu
   d. All of the above
   ANS: d
   OBJ: 3-7
   STO: MOUS PP2002 1-2
5. To copy a selected item, you can:
   a. Choose Copy from the shortcut menu
   b. Press [Ctrl]+[C]
   c. Click the Copy button
   d. All of the above
   ANS: d
   OBJ: 3-6
   STO: MOUS PP2002 2-2
6. The default design:
   a. Produces black text on a white background
   b. Produces shades of gray slides on a gray shaded background
   c. Provides shades of gray slides on a white background
   d. Provides a basic color scheme on a gray shaded background
   ANS: a
   OBJ: 3-1
   STO: MOUS PP2002 1-1
7. You can open the Color Scheme dialog box by using the:
   a. Format menu
   b. Color Scheme command on the Slide Design task pane
   c. Color Scheme button on the Formatting toolbar
   d. All of the above
   ANS: b
   OBJ: 3-5
   STO: MOUS PP2002 4-1
8. Speaker notes can consist of:
   a. A script
   b. Comments
   c. Reminders
   d. All of the above
   ANS: d
   OBJ: 3-8
   STO: MOUS PP2002 2-2
9. You can press [Ctrl]+[M] to:
   a. Change the slide layout
   b. Start a new presentation
   c. Demote text
   d. Insert a new slide
   ANS: d
   OBJ: 3-2
   STO: MOUS PP2002 1-2
10. You can apply new colors to the current design template by:
    a. Clicking the Color button on the Standard toolbar
    b. Pressing [Ctrl]+[W]
    c. Choosing Slide Color Scheme from the shortcut menu
    d. None of the above
    ANS: d
    OBJ: 3-5
    STO: MOUS PP2002 4-1
11. In a new slide, you can activate a placeholder by:
    a. Clicking it
    b. Pressing [Ctrl]+[Enter]
    c. a and b
    d. None of the above
    ANS: c
    OBJ: 3-3
    STO: MOUS PP2002 1-1
12. To demote a bullet, you can:
    a. Press [Tab]
    b. Click the Increase Indent button
    c. a and b
    d. None of the above
    ANS: c
    OBJ: 3-3
    STO: MOUS PP2002 2-2
13. If you press [Tab] or [Shift]+[Tab] when a bullet is selected, the text:
    a. Is demoted or promoted
    b. Moves forward or backward
    c. Is copied to the clipboard
    d. None of the above
    ANS: a
    OBJ: 3-3
    STO: MOUS PP2002 2-2
14. To undo the last action:
    a. Click the Undo button on the Common Tasks submenu
    b. Press [Ctrl]+[Z]
    c. Choose Undo from the Tools menu
    d. Press [Ctrl]+[Y]
    ANS: b
    OBJ: 3-4
    STO: MOUS PP2002 2-2
15. When you save a presentation, the Undo and Redo commands work as follows:
    a. They do nothing until you perform your next action
    b. They work as usual
    c. Undo works, but Redo isn't activated until an action is undone
    d. None of the above
    ANS: a
    OBJ: 3-4
    STO: MOUS PP2002 2-2
16. To cut a selected item, you can:
    a. Press [Ctrl]+[T]
    b. Choose Cut from the File menu

c. Click the Cut button
d. All of the above
ANS: c
OBJ: 3-6
STO: MOUS PP2002 2-2

17. The primary purpose of the Notes pane is to:
a. Create footnotes for slides as needed
b. Create notes for the speaker to use during the presentation
c. Change the order in which notes are presented
d. Create an outline along with explanatory notes
ANS: b
OBJ: 3-8
STO: MOUS PP2002 2-2

18. To demote text by using the [Tab] key, you must first:
a. Click the bullet to select all the text
b. Place an insertion point between the bullet and the text
c. a or b
d. None of the above
ANS: c
OBJ: 3-3
STO: MOUS PP2002 2-2

19. To remove a selected slide from the screen in Slide Sorter view and place it on the clipboard:
a. Press [Delete]
b. Click the Cut button
c. Press [Ctrl]+[C]
d. All of the above
ANS: b
OBJ: 3-6
STO: MOUS PP2002 4-8

20. The following is not true about the Notes pane:
a. It can be resized
b. Spelling cannot be checked
c. Text automatically wraps to a new line
d. It has a scroll bar
ANS: b
OBJ: 3-8
STO: MOUS PP2002 2-2

Completion

1. Moving a bulleted item up one level is called ____________________.
ANS: Promoting
OBJ: 3-3
STO: MOUS PP2002 2-2

2. Indenting a bulleted item to the right to make it a sub-bullet of a higher level is called ____________________.
ANS: Demoting
OBJ: 3-3
STO: MOUS PP2002 2-2

3. If you press [Tab] when the insertion point is within the text, you ____________________.
ANS: Insert a tab character
OBJ: 3-3
STO: MOUS PP2002 2-2

4. You can undo up to ____________________ actions (default setting).
ANS: 20
OBJ: 3-4
STO: MOUS PP2002 2-2

5. You can apply a design template by double-clicking a design name that appears on the ____________________ bar.
ANS: Status
OBJ: 3-5
STO: MOUS PP2002 1-1

6. The keyboard shortcut for Undo is ____________________.
ANS: [Ctrl]+[Z]
OBJ: 3-4
STO: MOUS PP2002 2-2

7. The keyboard shortcut for Redo is ____________________.
ANS: [Ctrl]+[Y]
OBJ: 3-4
STO: MOUS PP2002 2-2

8. To paste items, press ____________________.
ANS: [Ctrl]+[V]
OBJ: 3-6
STO: MOUS PP2002 2-2, 4-8

9. To restore the previous color scheme that you just changed, click the ____________________button.
ANS: Undo
OBJ: 3-4
STO: MOUS PP2002 2-2

10. You can apply a ____________________ to add a uniform color and design scheme to an entire presentation.
ANS: Design template
OBJ: 3-5
STO: MOUS PP2002 4-1

11. To apply a design template, choose Slide Design from the ____________________ menu.
ANS: Format
OBJ: 3-5
STO: MOUS PP2002 4-1

12. The Undo and Redo buttons are on the ____________________ toolbar.
ANS: Standard
OBJ: 3-4
STO: MOUS PP2002 2-2

13. In most cases, the first slide in a presentation uses the ____________________ AutoLayout.
ANS: Title Slide
OBJ: 3-7
STO: MOUS PP2002 4-4

14. To create a slide with two side-by-side bulleted lists, choose the ____________________ slide layout.
ANS: Title and 2-Column Text
OBJ: 3-7
STO: MOUS PP2002 4-4

15. To copy an item, select it and then press ____________________.
ANS: [Ctrl]+[C]
OBJ: 3-6
STO: MOUS PP2002 2-2, 4-8

16. The ____________________ is a Windows feature that stores multiple text or graphics items to use later.
ANS: Office Clipboard or Clipboard task pane
OBJ: 3-6
STO: MOUS PP2002 2-2, 4-8

17. In Normal view, the speaker Notes pane is located ____________________.
ANS: Below the Slide pane
OBJ: 3-8
STO: MOUS PP2002 2-2

18. To print speaker notes, you must change the entry in the ____________________ drop-down list on the Print dialog box.
ANS: Print What
OBJ: 3-8
STO: MOUS PP2002 5-1

19. To cut an item, select it and then press ___________ ________.
ANS: [Ctrl]+[X]
OBJ: 3-6
STO: MOUS PP2002 2-2, 4-8

20. When you create a blank presentation by clicking the New button, the design template that is automatically applied is named ________________.
ANS: Default design
OBJ: 3-1
STO: MOUS PP2002 1-1

Lesson 4: Outlines, Hyperlinks, and HTML

True/False

1. If the Outline tab is not displayed, to work in Outline format click the Normal View button and then the Outline tab.
ANS: T
OBJ: 4-1
STO: MOUS PP2002 1-1

2. When a title is demoted in the Outline pane, it becomes a new slide.
ANS: F
OBJ: 4-3
STO: MOUS PP2002 2-2

3. The Collapse All button on the Outlining toolbar displays only titles for the entire outline.
ANS: T
OBJ: 4-4
STO: MOUS PP2002 2-2

4. The Move Down button on the Outlining toolbar moves titles down one line at a time.
ANS: T
OBJ: 4-4
STO: MOUS PP2002 4-8

5. The first step in promoting or demoting items by dragging is to move the arrow pointer over the item until it becomes a four-pointed arrow.
ANS: T
OBJ: 4-4
STO: MOUS PP2002 4-8

6. You can use the Expand button in the Outline pane, the Slide pane, and Slide Sorter view.
ANS: F
OBJ: 4-4
STO: MOUS PP2002 4-8

7. When working in the Outline pane on a two-column slide layout, press [Alt]+[Spacebar] to access the second column.
ANS: F
OBJ: 4-2
STO: MOUS PP2002 4-4

8. If nothing is selected in the Outline pane, the Move Up and Move Down buttons apply their actions to the line containing the insertion point.
ANS: T
OBJ: 4-4
STO: MOUS PP2002 2-2

9. To move bulleted items within slides or between slides in the Outline pane, you can use the Cut and Paste commands.
ANS: T
OBJ: 4-4
STO: MOUS PP2002 2-2

10. When working in the Outline pane, you can combine two adjacent slides by demoting the second slide's title.
ANS: T
OBJ: 4-3
STO: MOUS PP2002 2-2

11. You must move bullets or slides individually when changing their positions.
ANS: F
OBJ: 4-4
STO: MOUS PP2002 4-8

12. If you move a collapsed slide, its hidden contents are not moved.
ANS: F
OBJ: 4-4
STO: MOUS PP2002 4-8

13. The Show Formatting button turns formatting on or off in both the Outline pane and the Slide pane.
ANS: F
OBJ: 4-4
STO: MOUS PP2002 2-2

14. If you click a bullet and then press [Delete] when working in the Outline pane, the bullet and all its sub-bullets will be deleted.
ANS: T
OBJ: 4-3
STO: MOUS PP2002 1-2

15. The Hypertext Markup Language file format is used to convert a PowerPoint presentation to a generic word processor document.
ANS: F
OBJ: 4-6
STO: MOUS PP2002 8-4

16. A hyperlink can be used to display an Excel spreadsheet during a slide show.
ANS: T
OBJ: 4-7
STO: MOUS PP2002 4-10

17. The keyboard shortcut [Ctrl]+[K] opens the Insert Hyperlink dialog box.
ANS: T
OBJ: 4-3
STO: MOUS PP2002 2-2

18. When working in the Outline pane, you can split one slide into two by promoting one of its bullets to the highest level.
ANS: T
OBJ: 4-3
STO: MOUS PP2002 2-2

19. If you import an outline from Word in which no heading styles are used, any text that is not indented becomes the title for a new slide.
ANS: T
OBJ: 4-5
STO: MOUS PP2002 2-1

20. The outline is the only element in a PowerPoint presentation that can be exported to a Word document.
ANS: F
OBJ: 4-5
STO: MOUS PP2002 2-1

Multiple Choice

1. To insert a new slide in the Outline pane:
   a. Press [Ctrl]+[Enter] at the end of a bulleted or subtitle line
   b. Press [Enter] at the end of a title line
   c. Click New Slide on the Formatting toolbar
   d. All of the above

ANS: d
OBJ: 4-2
STO: MOUS PP2002 1-2

2. The Expand button on the Outlining toolbar is used to:
   a. Increase the size of a slide
   b. Add more bulleted items to a slide
   c. Switch between showing only titles and showing all text
   d. Create a new slide for each item or paragraph on the current slide

   ANS: c
   OBJ: 4-4
   STO: MOUS PP2002 2-2

3. To promote or demote an entry:
   a. In the Slide pane, the insertion point must be positioned between the bullet and the text before using [Tab] or [Shift]+[Tab]
   b. In the Outline pane, you can click anywhere in an entry before demoting or promoting
   c. In the Outline pane, press [Tab] or [Shift]+[Tab]
   d. All of the above

   ANS: d
   OBJ: 4-3
   STO: MOUS PP2002 2-2

4. You can use the Expand All button in:
   a. The Outline pane, Slide pane, and Slide Sorter view only
   b. The Outline pane only
   c. The Slide pane or Outline pane only
   d. Slide Sorter view or the Outline pane only

   ANS: b
   OBJ: 4-4
   STO: MOUS PP2002 2-2

5. When working in the Outline pane, you can join two slides into one by:
   a. Dragging a sub-bullet to the left
   b. Placing the insertion point between a slide icon and the title text and then pressing [Shift]+[Tab]
   c. Dragging a slide icon to the right
   d. Dragging a slide icon up

   ANS: c
   OBJ: 4-3
   STO: MOUS PP2002 2-2

6. HTML is an acronym for:
   a. Hypertext Makeover Logic
   b. Hypertext Move Locator
   c. Hypertext Markup Language
   d. Help Topic Management Language

   ANS: c
   OBJ: 4-6
   STO: MOUS PP2002 8-4

7. To move bulleted items within slides or between slides in the Outline pane, you can:
   a. Choose Move Up or Move Down from the Edit menu
   b. Drag selected bullets up or down
   c. Press the [Up Arrow] or [Down Arrow] keys
   d. None of the above

   ANS: b
   OBJ: 4-4
   STO: MOUS PP2002 2-2

8. When dragging a bullet, the indicator for moving text up or down is:
   a. A two-pointed vertical arrow
   b. A four-pointed arrow
   c. A single-pointed arrow
   d. A two-pointed horizontal arrow

   ANS: a
   OBJ: 4-4
   STO: MOUS PP2002 2-2

9. When importing an outline into PowerPoint:
   a. You can import only Microsoft Word outlines
   b. The file to be imported must be open
   c. You can import into a blank presentation or one that already contains slides
   d. All of the above

   ANS: c
   OBJ: 4-4
   STO: MOUS PP2002 2-1

10. One of the advantages of working in the Outline pane is that:
    a. A new slide is automatically created if you key too much text
    b. You can concentrate on the textual content without being distracted by the graphics
    c. Content is automatically suggested for your presentation
    d. The style checker works only in the Outline pane

    ANS: b
    OBJ: 4-1
    STO: MOUS PP2002 1-1

11. To turn Show Formatting on or off:
    a. Press [Alt]+[Shift]+[A]
    b. Press [Alt]+[Shift]+[front slash (/)] on the numeric keyboard
    c. Press [front slash (/)] on the numeric keyboard
    d. None of the above

    ANS: a
    OBJ: 4-4
    STO: MOUS PP2002 2-2

12. To move items up in an outline, press:
    a. [Up Arrow]
    b. [Shift]+[Up Arrow]
    c. [Alt]+[Shift]+[Up Arrow]
    d. None of the above

    ANS: c
    OBJ: 4-4
    STO: MOUS PP2002 2-2

13. After slide text is collapsed, you can use the Expand button to expand the text by first placing the insertion point:
    a. At the end of the previous slide
    b. Within the slide's bulleted text
    c. In the slide title
    d. None of the above

    ANS: c
    OBJ: 4-4
    STO: MOUS PP2002 2-2

14. To demote an item, you can:
    a. Click the Demote button
    b. Click the Decrease Indent button on the Formatting toolbar
    c. Press [Shift]+[Tab]
    d. All of the above

    ANS: a
    OBJ: 4-3
    STO: MOUS PP2002 2-2

15. The fastest way to print the outline of a PowerPoint presentation is to:
    a. Select all the outline text and then click the Print button on the Standard toolbar
    b. Click the Preview button on the Standard toolbar and then choose Outline View in the Print What list box
    c. From the File menu, choose Send to, Microsoft Word and then print the resulting Word document
    d. Click the Print Outline button on the Outlining toolbar

    ANS: b
    OBJ: 4-4
    STO: MOUS PP2002 5-1

16. When creating a Word outline, you can indicate slide titles and bullets by using:
    a. Tabs
    b. Indents
    c. Heading styles
    d. All of the above
    ANS: d
    OBJ: 4-5
    STO: MOUS PP2002 2-1
17. To use a hyperlink that links to another file:
    a. You must first save the presentation as a Web page
    b. Run a slide show
    c. Make sure the linked file is saved in HTML format
    d. If the linked file is a Word document, make sure it's in outline format
    ANS: b
    OBJ: 4-7
    STO: MOUS PP2002 4-10
18. When you click a bullet with the four-pointed arrow:
    a. All bullets at the same level are selected
    b. Only the line that contains the bullet is selected
    c. The line that contains the bullet and all the lower-level bullets below it are selected
    d. You can click only a slide icon with the four-pointed arrow
    ANS: c
    OBJ: 4-4
    STO: MOUS PP2002 2-2
19. To send a PowerPoint outline to Word:
    a. The Outline pane must be active
    b. The outline text that you want to send must be selected
    c. The Show Formatting button must be turned on to preserve the formatting
    d. None of the above
    ANS: d
    OBJ: 4-5
    STO: MOUS PP2002 5-1
20. When you import an outline from Word:
    a. The text formatting is determined by the Word document
    b. The PowerPoint design template determines the text formatting
    c. You can choose whether to preserve the Word document text formatting
    d. Word document text formatting is preserved only if you used Heading styles to create the document
    ANS: b
    OBJ: 4-5
    STO: MOUS PP2002 2-1

Completion

1. When you promote a first-level bullet in the Outline pane, it becomes a __________________.
   ANS: New slide
   OBJ: 4-3
   STO: MOUS PP2002 2-2
2. To preview a presentation as a Web page, you can choose Web Page Preview from the ______________ _____ menu.
   ANS: File
   OBJ: 4-6
   STO: MOUS PP2002 8-4
3. To change the width of the Outline pane, _________ ________________.
   ANS: Drag its right border
   OBJ: 4-1
   STO: MOUS PP2002 2-2
4. In a long outline, click the __________________ button to make it easier to move slides by displaying only the slide titles.
   ANS: Collapse All
   OBJ: 4-4
   STO: MOUS PP2002 2-2
5. To make it easier to read the text of an outline, click the __________________ button to turn off formatting applied by a template.
   ANS: Show Formatting
   OBJ: 4-4
   STO: MOUS PP2002 2-2
6. To insert a Word outline into PowerPoint, choose the Slides from Outline command from the __________ ________ menu.
   ANS: Insert
   OBJ: 4-5
   STO: MOUS PP2002 2-1
7. Besides importing Word outlines into PowerPoint, you can also __________________ PowerPoint outlines to Word.
   ANS: Export or Send
   OBJ: 4-5
   STO: MOUS PP2002 6-4
8. To show titles only for selected slides, click the _____ _____________ button.
   ANS: Collapse
   OBJ: 4-4
   STO: MOUS PP2002 2-2
9. To restore previous positioning of an item, click the __________________ button.
   ANS: Undo
   OBJ: 4-4
   STO: MOUS PP2002 4-8
10. To Expand all outline items, press ______________ ____.
    ANS: [Alt]+[Shift]+[1]
    OBJ: 4-4
    STO: MOUS PP2002 4-8
11. When working in the Outline pane, you can insert a new slide by pressing __________________ at the end of a title line.
    ANS: [Enter]
    OBJ: 4-2
    STO: MOUS PP2002 1-2
12. When working in the Outline pane, you can insert a new slide by pressing __________________ at the end of a bulleted or subtitle line.
    ANS: [Ctrl]+[M]
    OBJ: 4-2
    STO: MOUS PP2002 1-2
13. When you demote a title, it becomes a ___________ ____________________________.
    ANS: Bulleted item on the previous slide
    OBJ: 4-3
    STO: MOUS PP2002 2-2
14. To delete a slide in the Outline pane, click its slide icon and then press __________________.
    ANS: [Delete]
    OBJ: 4-3
    STO: MOUS PP2002 1-2
15. If you choose Delete Slide from the Edit menu when working in the Outline pane, the slide that has the __________________ anywhere in its title or bullets will be deleted.
    ANS: Insertion point

OBJ: 4-3
STO: MOUS PP2002 1-2

16. When an insertion point is in the middle of a slide's title in the Outline pane, use the keyboard shortcut __________ to insert a new slide.
ANS: [Ctrl]+[M]
OBJ: 4-2
STO: MOUS PP2002 1-2

17. The generic name for a software program that you can use to view a presentation or other document saved as a Web page is called a __________.
ANS: Browser
OBJ: 4-6
STO: MOUS PP2002 8-4

18. To select an entire slide in the Outline pane, click its __________ with the four-pointed arrow.
ANS: Slide icon
OBJ: 4-4
STO: MOUS PP2002 4-8

19. You can adjust the magnification of text in the Outline pane for easy viewing by using the __________ feature.
ANS: Zoom
OBJ: 4-1
STO: MOUS PP2002 2-2

20. The button on the Outlining toolbar that has a plus sign is named the __________ button.
ANS: Expand
OBJ: 4-4
STO: MOUS PP2002 2-2

Lesson 5: Working with Text

True/False

1. You can choose text attributes, such as bold, only after selecting text.
ANS: F
OBJ: 5-1
STO: MOUS PP2002 2-2

2. You can change text attributes in both the Slide pane and the Outline pane.
ANS: T
OBJ: 5-1
STO: MOUS PP2002 2-2

3. You can use one of the Content slide layouts to create a table.
ANS: T
OBJ: 5-6
STO: MOUS PP2002 3-1

4. Fonts containing potential bullet characters include Symbol, Wingdings, and Webdings.
ANS: T
OBJ: 5-4
STO: MOUS PP2002 2-2

5. You can open the Bullets and Numbering dialog box by using the shortcut menu.
ANS: T
OBJ: 5-4
STO: MOUS PP2002 2-2

6. The slide master includes text placeholders for the title and subtitle of a slide.
ANS: F
OBJ: 5-8
STO: MOUS PP2002 4-1

7. You format a placeholder on a master slide in the same way as you format a placeholder on a slide.
ANS: T
OBJ: 5-8
STO: MOUS PP2002 4-1

8. Title and slide masters make it easy to create consistently formatted presentations.
ANS: T
OBJ: 5-8
STO: MOUS PP2002 4-1

9. You can select an entire table by double-clicking a corner table cell.
ANS: F
OBJ: 5-6
STO: MOUS PP2002 3-1

10. Changing a master automatically overrides all earlier changes you made to individual slides.
ANS: F
OBJ: 5-8
STO: MOUS PP2002 4-1

11. When master slides are displayed, placeholders for the date, footer, and slide number appear.
ANS: T
OBJ: 5-8
STO: MOUS PP2002 4-1

12. You can change text color by pressing [Shift]+[C].
ANS: F
OBJ: 5-8
STO: MOUS PP2002 2-2

13. You can use a corner-sizing handle to change both the height and width of a text box.
ANS: T
OBJ: 5-7
STO: MOUS PP2002 4-9

14. The Formatting toolbar contains buttons for left aligning, right aligning, or centering text.
ANS: T
OBJ: 5-5
STO: MOUS PP2002 2-2

15. To open the Replace Font dialog box, choose Replace Fonts from the Format menu.
ANS: T
OBJ: 5-1
STO: MOUS PP2002 2-2

16. The Replace Font dialog box enables you to replace fonts for an entire presentation or just one slide.
ANS: F
OBJ: 5-1
STO: MOUS PP2002 2-2

17. The keyboard shortcut for center-aligning text is [Ctrl]l+[C].
ANS: F
OBJ: 5-5
STO: MOUS PP2002 2-2

18. Auto-numbered bullets cannot be formatted with Roman numerals. If you want to use Roman numerals, you must key them individually.
ANS: F
OBJ: 5-4
STO: MOUS PP2002 2-2

19. When an insertion point is active in a table, you can move from cell to cell by using [Tab] and [Shift]+[Tab].
ANS: T
OBJ: 5-6
STO: MOUS PP2002 3-1

20. You can insert a column only to the left of the selected column and insert a row only above the selected row.
ANS: F
OBJ: 5-6
STO: MOUS PP2002 3-1

Multiple Choice

1. To deselect a placeholder or other object, press:
a. [Backspace] one or more times
b. [Esc] one or more times
c. [Spacebar] one or more times
d. All of the above
ANS: b
OBJ: 5-3
STO: MOUS PP2002 2-2

2. To select placeholders and text boxes:
a. Press [Esc] while a placeholder has an insertion point
b. Press [Tab] (when an insertion point is not active on the slide) to select the next object on the slide
c. Click the border of an active placeholder with the arrow pointer
d. All of the above
ANS: d
OBJ: 5-3
STO: MOUS PP2002 2-2

3. TrueType fonts:
a. Appear with a printer icon to the left in the Font drop-down list on the Formatting toolbar
b. Can be printed only on a specific printer
c. Can be formatted in a variety of colors
d. Have a very limited range of font sizes
ANS: c
OBJ: 5-1
STO: MOUS PP2002 2-2

4. You can change the size and position of text placeholders by:
a. Dragging the text box border to move the text
b. Dragging a sizing handle to change the size and shape of the text placeholder
c. Using the Format AutoShape dialog box
d. All of the above
ANS: d
OBJ: 5-7
STO: MOUS PP2002 4-9

5. To be successful in dragging a text placeholder to a new position, the pointer must be positioned on its border in such a way that it changes to:
a. A four-pointed arrow
b. A two-pointed arrow
c. A single arrow
d. None of the above
ANS: a
OBJ: 5-7
STO: MOUS PP2002 4-9

6. To display the slide and title masters, you can:
a. Use the View menu
b. Hold down [Shift] and click the Slide Show button
c. Click the Masters button on the Formatting toolbar
d. None of the above
ANS: a
OBJ: 5-8
STO: MOUS PP2002 4-1

7. You can switch ("toggle") between the title master and slide master by:
a. Using the vertical scroll bar
b. Using the View menu
c. Pressing [Alt]+[Up Arrow] or [Alt]+[Down Arrow]
d. All of the above
ANS: a
OBJ: 5-8
STO: MOUS PP2002 4-1

8. You can use the following feature to ensure that master slide formatting is applied to all previously individually formatted slides:
a. AutoFormat
b. Reapply Layout
c. Repeat command
d. None of the above
ANS: b
OBJ: 5-8
STO: MOUS PP2002 4-1

9. To move to the previous cell in a table, press:
a. [Backspace]
b. [Tab]
c. [Shift]+[Tab]
d. None of the above
ANS: c
OBJ: 5-6
STO: MOUS PP2002 3-1

10. Pressing [Tab] in a table's cell:
a. Can change the height of the cell
b. Moves the insertion point to the next cell
c. Has no effect
d. None of the above
ANS: b
OBJ: 5-6
STO: MOUS PP2002 3-1

11. To center-align text:
a. Press [Ctrl]+[C]
b. Press [Ctrl]+[E]
c. Press [Ctrl]+[M]
d. None of the above
ANS: b
OBJ: 5-5
STO: MOUS PP2002 2-2

12. To justify text:
a. Click the Justify button on the Formatting toolbar
b. Press [Shift]+[J]
c. Choose Alignment from the Format menu
d. Choose Spacing from the Format menu
ANS: c
OBJ: 5-5
STO: MOUS PP2002 2-2

13. To make selected text bold, press:
a. [Shift]+[B]
b. [Ctrl]+[B]
c. [Alt]+[B]
d. None of the above
ANS: b
OBJ: 5-1
STO: MOUS PP2002 2-2

14. To apply a text shadow:
a. Click the Shadow button on the Formatting toolbar
b. Press [Ctrl]+[S]
c. Press [Shift]+[S]
d. None of the above
ANS: a
OBJ: 5-1
STO: MOUS PP2002 2-2

15. To change the size of a text box, you can:
    a. Key the height and width measurements in the Slide Layout task pane
    b. Drag one of the white sizing handles
    c. Press [Ctrl]+[>] repeatedly
    d. Press [Ctrl]+[Up Arrow] repeatedly
    ANS: b
    OBJ: 5-7
    STO: MOUS PP2002 4-9

16. To quickly change the color of all the first-level bullets in a presentation:
    a. Choose the Bullet Color option in the Replace Fonts dialog box
    b. Select the first-level bulleted line on the slide master and then open the Bullets and Numbering dialog box
    c. Right-click the bulleted line on the slide master and then choose Bullet Color from the shortcut menu
    d. Select the bullet on the slide master and then click the Font Color button
    ANS: b
    OBJ: 5-4
    STO: MOUS PP2002 2-2

17. To change the color of a single word in a text box:
    a. Right-click the word and then choose Text Color from the shortcut menu
    b. Double-click the word, open the Font dialog box, and click the Color arrow
    c. Double-click the word and then click the Fill Color button
    d. a or b
    ANS: b
    OBJ: 5-1
    STO: MOUS PP2002 2-2

18. To italicize a word:
    a. Double-click the word and then press [Ctrl]+[I]
    b. Place the insertion point somewhere within the word and then click the Italic button
    c. Click the Italic button, key the word, and then click the Italic button again
    d. All of the above
    ANS: d
    OBJ: 5-1
    STO: MOUS PP2002 2-2

19. To use the Replace Fonts feature:
    a. Click the Replace Fonts tab on the Font dialog box
    b. Choose Replace Fonts from the Format menu
    c. Select a word containing the font to be replaced and then choose Replace Fonts from the shortcut menu
    d. Choose Replace Fonts from the Tools menu
    ANS: b
    OBJ: 5-1
    STO: MOUS PP2002 2-2

20. When you click the Center button on the Formatting toolbar:
    a. The active text box is automatically centered on the slide
    b. If text is selected, all the text in that bulleted line or title line is centered within its text box
    c. If the text-box border is selected, but no text within the text box is selected, nothing happens
    d. None of the above
    ANS: b
    OBJ: 5-5
    STO: MOUS PP2002 2-2

Completion

1. You can cycle through uppercase, lowercase, and title case by selecting the text and pressing ____________________.
   ANS: [Shift]+[F3]
   OBJ: 5-1
   STO: MOUS PP2002 2-2

2. Arial and Times New Roman are types of ____________________.
   ANS: Fonts
   OBJ: 5-1
   STO: MOUS PP2002 2-2

3. A ____________________ displays data in rows and columns.
   ANS: Table
   OBJ: 5-6
   STO: MOUS PP2002 3-1

4. ____________________ are the eight small white circles along the border of a selected placeholder that you use to change the placeholder's size and shape.
   ANS: Sizing handles
   OBJ: 5-8
   STO: MOUS PP2002 4-1

5. A ____________________ contains formatted text placeholders and background items that appear on all slides in a presentation.
   ANS: Master slide
   OBJ: 5-7
   STO: MOUS PP2002 2-4

6. To increase font size, you can press ____________________ on the keyboard.
   ANS: [Ctrl]+[Shift]+[>]
   OBJ: 5-1
   STO: MOUS PP2002 2-2

7. To italicize text, you can press ____________________ on the keyboard.
   ANS: [Ctrl]+[I]
   OBJ: 5-1
   STO: MOUS PP2002 2-2

8. You can change font color by clicking the Font Color button on the ____________________ toolbar.
   ANS: Drawing or Formatting
   OBJ: 5-1
   STO: MOUS PP2002 2-2

9. Points refer to a font's ____________________.
   ANS: Size or Height
   OBJ: 5-1
   STO: MOUS PP2002 2-2

10. Press ____________________ to close the Font drop-down list on the Formatting toolbar without choosing a font.
    ANS: Esc or The Font drop-down list arrow
    OBJ: 5-1
    STO: MOUS PP2002 2-2

11. The ____________________ Case option changes uppercase letters to lowercase letters and lowercase letters to uppercase letters.
    ANS: Toggle
    OBJ: 5-1
    STO: MOUS PP2002 2-2

12. To open the Bullets and Numbering dialog box, right-click a text line and choose Bullets and Numbering from the ____________________ menu.
    ANS: Shortcut
    OBJ: 5-4
    STO: MOUS PP2002 2-2

13. To underline text, you can press ________________ __ on the keyboard.
ANS: [Ctrl]+[U]
OBJ: 5-1
STO: MOUS PP2002 2-2

14. An easy way to add another row to a table is to move the pointer to the right-most cell in the last row of the table and press __________________.
ANS: [Tab]
OBJ: 5.6
STO: MOUS PP2002 3-1

15. To enlarge both the height and width of a text box simultaneously, drag a ______________________.
ANS: Corner sizing handle
OBJ: 5-7
STO: MOUS PP2002 4-9

16. In a table, each data item, label, heading, or number is entered into a __________________, which is the box formed by the intersection of a row and column.
ANS: Cell
OBJ: 5.6
STO: MOUS PP2002 3-1

17. To create a numbered list, choose ________________ _______ from the Format menu.
ANS: Bullets and Numbering
OBJ: 5-4
STO: MOUS PP2002 2-2

18. To right-align selected text, you can use the keyboard shortcut __________________.
ANS: [Ctrl]+[R]
OBJ: 5-5
STO: MOUS PP2002 2-2

19. To make selected text bold, you can use the keyboard shortcut __________________.
ANS: [Ctrl]+[B]
OBJ: 5-1
STO: MOUS PP2002 2-2

20. Click the __________________ tab on the Format AutoShape dialog box to make a text box smaller.
ANS: Size
OBJ: 5-7
STO: MOUS PP2002 4-9

Lesson 6: Working with PowerPoint Objects

True/False

1. You can open the Format Picture dialog box by right-clicking a picture, such as clip art, and choosing Format Picture.
ANS: T
OBJ: 6-4
STO: MOUS PP2002 3-1

2. You can use the Formatting toolbar to control various aspects of an image's appearance, such as brightness, contrast, and color.
ANS: F
OBJ: 6-4
STO: MOUS PP2002 3-1

3. Text created as a WordArt image is checked for spelling errors whenever you use the spell-checker.
ANS: F
OBJ: 6-5
STO: MOUS PP2002 3-3

4. You can use the slide master to add drawing objects and clip art to every slide in a presentation.
ANS: T
OBJ: 6-4
STO: MOUS PP2002 3-2

5. You can press the [Delete] key to delete a selected drawn object created with a drawing tool such as the Rectangle tool.
ANS: T
OBJ: 6-1
STO: MOUS PP2002 3-3

6. Double-clicking a drawing tool, such as the Line tool, enables you to draw multiple lines as needed.
ANS: T
OBJ: 6-1
STO: MOUS PP2002 3-3

7. Some AutoShapes include a yellow diamond handle for reshaping objects after they are drawn.
ANS: T
OBJ: 6-2
STO: MOUS PP2002 3-3

8. If the AutoShape menu is in your way, the only way to solve this problem is to close it by clicking the Close button in the upper-left corner of the toolbar.
ANS: F
OBJ: 6-2
STO: MOUS PP2002 3-3

9. You can add text to an AutoShape by using the Cut and Paste commands or by keying in the text directly.
ANS: T
OBJ: 6-2
STO: MOUS PP2002 3-3

10. When keying text in a rotated object, clicking the I-beam causes the object and text to rotate to a horizontal position for easy text editing.
ANS: T
OBJ: 6-7
STO: MOUS PP2002 2-2

11. You can use the arrow keys to change the position of a selected object.
ANS: T
OBJ: 6-1
STO: MOUS PP2002 3-3

12. You cannot use the Copy and Paste commands with clip art or AutoShapes.
ANS: F
OBJ: 6-3
STO: MOUS PP2002 3-1

13. You can click the Undo button to undo the resizing of a drawn object.
ANS: T
OBJ: 6-1
STO: MOUS PP2002 3-3

14. You move WordArt objects the same way you move clip art images.
ANS: T
OBJ: 6-5
STO: MOUS PP2002 3-3

15. When drawing a text box, you must drag it to the correct size to accommodate the text you want to key.
ANS: F
OBJ: 6-6
STO: MOUS PP2002 2-2

16. The Insert Clip Art button is on the Standard toolbar.
ANS: F
OBJ: 6-3
STO: MOUS PP2002 3-1

17. Clicking the Insert Clip Art button opens the Insert Clip Art task pane.
ANS: T
OBJ: 6-3
STO: MOUS PP2002 3-1

18. If you try to key text when an AutoShape is selected, you will get an error message.
ANS: F
OBJ: 6-2
STO: MOUS PP2002 3-3

19. An AutoShape's adjustment handle is the small green circle that appears near an AutoShape when it is selected.
ANS: F
OBJ: 6-2
STO: MOUS PP2002 3-3

20. PowerPoint provides tools to adjust the contrast and brightness of a scanned image.
ANS: T
OBJ: 6-4
STO: MOUS PP2002 3-1

Multiple Choice

1. To insert clip art:
   a. Click the Insert Clip Art button on the Standard toolbar or choose Clip Art from the Insert menu
   b. Click the Insert Clip Art button on the Drawing toolbar or choose Clip Art from the Insert menu
   c. Click the Insert Clip Art button on the Formatting toolbar or choose Clip Art from the Format menu
   d. None of the above
ANS: b
OBJ: 6-3
STO: MOUS PP2002 3-1

2. The indicator for moving an object or text without resizing is:
   a. A dotted outline
   b. A two-pointed arrow
   c. The I-beam
   d. A four-pointed arrow
ANS: d
OBJ: 6-1
STO: MOUS PP2002 3-3

3. To deactivate the cropping tool:
   a. Press [Esc]
   b. Click anywhere outside the image
   c. Click the cropping tool on the Picture toolbar
   d. All of the above
ANS: d
OBJ: 6-4
STO: MOUS PP2002 3-1

4. The best way to place additional text outside a text placeholder is to:
   a. Copy and Paste a title placeholder and then move and resize it
   b. Draw a text box by clicking the Text Box button on the Drawing toolbar
   c. Choose Text Box from the Edit menu
   d. b or c
ANS: b
OBJ: 6-6
STO: MOUS PP2002 2-2

5. You can rotate:
   a. All PowerPoint objects
   b. Text boxes but not WordArt
   c. AutoShapes but not clip art
   d. Bitmaps but not vector images
ANS: a
OBJ: 6-7
STO: MOUS PP2002 3-3

6. The AutoShape menu contains submenus for:
   a. Clip Art
   b. Block Arrows
   c. WordArt
   d. All of the above
ANS: b
OBJ: 6-2
STO: MOUS PP2002 3-3

7. When drawing a constrained object, you hold down the following key(s):
   a. [Ctrl]
   b. [Ctrl]+[C]
   c. [Shift]
   d. [Alt]
ANS: c
OBJ: 6-1
STO: MOUS PP2002 3-3

8. To make an object shrink or grow from the center rather than the side, you:
   a. Double-click the object with the right mouse button
   b. Triple-click the object
   c. Hold down [Ctrl]
   d. None of the above
ANS: c
OBJ: 6-1
STO: MOUS PP2002 3-3

9. You click the Lock Aspect Ratio option to:
   a. Prevent an image from being moved
   b. Prevent an image from being sized
   c. Ensure that the height and width of an image are resized proportionately
   d. None of the above
ANS: c
OBJ: 6-1
STO: MOUS PP2002 3-3

10. Which type of sizing handle do you drag to change a clip art image's original proportions:
    a. Any sizing handle
    b. Corner handles
    c. Yellow handles
    d. Side handles
ANS: d
OBJ: 6-4
STO: MOUS PP2002 3-1

11. Which menu contains predefined shapes that you can use in your presentations:
    a. AutoShapes
    b. AutoForms
    c. Drawing
    d. All of the above
ANS: a
OBJ: 6-2
STO: MOUS PP2002 3-3

12. You use the Rectangle button on the Drawing toolbar to:
    a. Draw rectangles only
    b. Draw squares and rectangles
    c. Draw any straight-sided object
    d. Select rectangles and squares
ANS: b
OBJ: 6-1
STO: MOUS PP2002 3-3

13. To change an existing AutoShape to a different shape while preserving the size, position, and rotation angle of the original:
    a. Select the original AutoShape and then use the AutoShape button to draw a new shape

b. Select the original AutoShape and then choose Change AutoShape from the Draw menu
c. Right-click the AutoShape and then choose Format AutoShape from the shortcut menu
d. Delete the existing AutoShape and draw a new one from scratch
ANS: b
OBJ: 6-2
STO: MOUS PP2002 3-3

14. When a clip art image is selected, the Picture toolbar enables you to:
a. Adjust the brightness and contrast of the picture
b. Replace the picture with a different one
c. Copy the picture to another slide
d. All of the above
ANS: a
OBJ: 6-4
STO: MOUS PP2002 3-1

15. A constrained line is a line:
a. Within a fixed-width text box
b. That is set to a predefined thickness
c. That is exactly horizontal, vertical, or at a multiple of a 15-degree angle
d. None of the above
ANS: c
OBJ: 6-1
STO: MOUS PP2002 3-3

16. To place text inside an AutoShape:
a. Select the shape and then key the text
b. Select the shape and then choose Text from the Insert menu
c. Right-click the shape and then key the text
d. a or b
ANS: a
OBJ: 6-2
STO: MOUS PP2002 3-3

17. If you click the Text Box tool once on the slide and the text that you key becomes a thin vertical column of characters:
a. You accidentally dragged the Text Box tool while you clicked it
b. You tried to place the text box in an invalid place
c. The text box is too close to the right edge of the slide
d. You can fix it by pressing [Ctrl]+[Right] Arrow
ANS: a
OBJ: 6-6
STO: MOUS PP2002 2-2

18. You can crop a picture by:
a. Clicking the Crop tab on the Format Picture dialog box
b. Dragging a cropping handle with the cropping tool
c. Clicking the Size tab on the Format Picture dialog box
d. b or c
ANS: b
OBJ: 6-4
STO: MOUS PP2002 3-1

19. The following option(s) can be set on the Insert Clip Art task pane:
a. Collections to search
b. Search text
c. Media type to search
d. All of the above
ANS: d
OBJ: 6-3
STO: MOUS PP2002 3-1

20. The following types of objects can be rotated:
a. AutoShapes
b. Thumbnails
c. Slides
d. a and b
ANS: a
OBJ: 6-7
STO: MOUS PP2002 3-3

Completion

1. PowerPoint provides expertly drawn pictures called ________________ that you can insert in your presentations.
ANS: Clip art
OBJ: 6-3
STO: MOUS PP2002 3-1

2. When you control the drawing or movement of an object in precise increments or proportions, so as to create a perfect circle or square, you are creating a ________________ object.
ANS: Constrained
OBJ: 6-1
STO: MOUS PP2002 3-3

3. After you click the Search button on the Insert Clip Art task pane, small images called ________________ appear.
ANS: Thumbnails
OBJ: 6-3
STO: MOUS PP2002 3-1

4. Changing the size of an object, such as clip art, while maintaining the relationship between the height and width of the object is called ________________.
ANS: Proportional sizing or Locking the aspect ratio
OBJ: 6-4
STO: MOUS PP2002 3-1

5. Cutting off part of a graphic image, similar to cutting off part of a picture by using scissors, is called ________________.
ANS: Cropping
OBJ: 6-4
STO: MOUS PP2002 3-1

6. When you rotate a text object, holding down the [Shift] key enables you to rotate in precise increments of ________________ degrees.
ANS: 15
OBJ: 6-7
STO: MOUS PP2002 2-2

7. A large number of clip art images not stored on your local system are available in the Insert Clip Art task pane if ________________.
ANS: You are connected to the Internet
OBJ: 6-3
STO: MOUS PP2002 3-1

8. To see a menu of options for a clip art image, right-click ________________.
ANS: Its thumbnail
OBJ: 6-3
STO: MOUS PP2002 3.1

9. To resize WordArt proportionately, you must hold down the ________________ key while you drag a corner handle.
ANS: [Shift]
OBJ: 6-5
STO: MOUS PP2002 3-3

10. Keying a negative number in the Rotation text box rotates an image in a ________________ direction.

ANS: Counterclockwise
OBJ: 6-7
STO: MOUS PP2002 3-3

11. A clip art image made up of a large number of tiny colored dots is called a ________________.
ANS: Bitmap
OBJ: 6-3
STO: MOUS PP2002 3-1

12. Tools used to modify clip art are located on the ________________ toolbar.
ANS: Picture
OBJ: 6-4
STO: MOUS PP2002 3-1

13. WordArt tools are located on the ________________ toolbar.
ANS: WordArt
OBJ: 6-5
STO: MOUS PP2002 3-3

14. The AutoShapes button is located on the ________________ toolbar.
ANS: Drawing
OBJ: 6-2
STO: MOUS PP2002 3-3

15. To place text in an AutoShape, select the AutoShape and then ________________.
ANS: Key the text
OBJ: 6-2
STO: MOUS PP2002 3-3

16. If you drag a top center-sizing handle up on an AutoShape, you will make it ________________.
ANS: Taller or Higher
OBJ: 6-2
STO: MOUS PP2002 3-3

17. To distort a clip art image by making it wider without changing its height, drag ________________.
ANS: A left- or right-side sizing handle
OBJ: 6-4
STO: MOUS PP2002 3-1

18. You can easily change the shape of a WordArt object by clicking the WordArt Shape button on the ________________ toolbar.
ANS: WordArt
OBJ: 6-5
STO: MOUS PP2002 3-3

19. If the Picture toolbar is not showing, choose ________________ from the View menu and then choose Picture.
ANS: Toolbars
OBJ: 6-4
STO: MOUS PP2002 3-1

20. To draw a circle, click ________________ on the Drawing toolbar and then hold down the [Shift] key while dragging.
ANS: Oval
OBJ: 6-1
STO: MOUS PP2002 3-3

Lesson 7: Working with Lines, Fills, and Colors

True/False

1. You have a choice of several dash styles when adding a border to a text placeholder.
ANS: T
OBJ: 7-1
STO: MOUS PP2002 4-1

2. To change the line color of an object's border, click the Line Type button on the Drawing toolbar.
ANS: F
OBJ: 7-1
STO: MOUS PP2002 4-1

3. You use the same overall technique to change the color of a line as you do to change the color of an object border.
ANS: T
OBJ: 7-1
STO: MOUS PP2002 4-1

4. You can preview a line-color change if you use the Format AutoShape dialog box.
ANS: T
OBJ: 7-1
STO: MOUS PP2002 4-1

5. You can change the fill color of an object by choosing Format AutoShape from the shortcut menu or by clicking the Fill Color button on the Drawing toolbar.
ANS: T
OBJ: 7-2
STO: MOUS PP2002 3-3

6. Fill colors and border lines can be removed from an object simultaneously.
ANS: F
OBJ: 7-2
STO: MOUS PP2002 3-3

7. Square Dot and Round Dot are examples of dash-line styles.
ANS: T
OBJ: 7-1
STO: MOUS PP2002 4-1

8. Preset is a color option when working with gradient fills.
ANS: T
OBJ: 7-4
STO: MOUS PP2002 4-4

9. "Follow fills scheme color" is an example of a ScreenTip that identifies one of the standard colors in a presentation color scheme.
ANS: T
OBJ: 7-3
STO: MOUS PP2002 4-4

10. When applying a gradient fill to a text box, the text color changes automatically if needed to preserve legibility.
ANS: F
OBJ: 7-4
STO: MOUS PP2002 4-4

11. When adding a textured fill to an object, the name of the texture appears under the textured fill patterns on the Texture tab of the Fill Effects dialog box.
ANS: T
OBJ: 7-4
STO: MOUS PP2002 4-4

12. You cannot apply a fill effect to a master-slide object.
ANS: F
OBJ: 7-4
STO: MOUS PP2002 4-4

13. To use a fill color that is not one of the color scheme colors, you need to choose a different color scheme.
ANS: F
OBJ: 7.3
STO: MOUS PP2002 4-4

14. Line weight is the thickness of a line measured in points.
ANS: T
OBJ: 7-1
STO: MOUS PP2002 4-1

15. Grayscale settings are available only when Grayscale view is displayed.
ANS: T
OBJ: 7-6
STO: MOUS PP2002 4-1

16. There are hundreds of fill pattern styles that you can apply using a variety of color combinations.
ANS: F
OBJ: 7-2
STO: MOUS PP2002 3-3

17. The Format Painter tool is used to repeat your last action.
ANS: F
OBJ: 7-5
STO: MOUS PP2002 4-1

18. Transparency settings are not available for preset gradient fills.
ANS: F
OBJ: 7-3
STO: MOUS PP2002 4-1

19. When you use a picture fill, you are limited to pictures stored in the Clip Art Gallery.
ANS: F
OBJ: 7-4
STO: MOUS PP2002 4-4

20. You can change both the size and the style of arrowheads.
ANS: T
OBJ: 7-1
STO: MOUS PP2002 4-1

Multiple Choice

1. To add a border to a text placeholder:
a. Choose Colors and Lines from the Format menu
b. Choose Borders from the Insert menu
c. Click the Add a Border button on the Drawing toolbar
d. None of the above
ANS: d
OBJ: 7-1
STO: MOUS PP2002 4-1

2. You can add an arrowhead to a selected straight line by:
a. Clicking the Add Arrow button on the Drawing toolbar
b. Choosing Colors and Lines from the Format menu
c. Choosing AutoShape from the Format menu
d. All of the above
ANS: c
OBJ: 7-1
STO: MOUS PP2002 4-1

3. To adjust the length and angle of an arrow:
a. Drag its tail with the single-headed arrow
b. Drag its tail with the two-pointed arrow
c. Drag its tail with the four-pointed arrow
d. None of the above
ANS: b
OBJ: 7-1
STO: MOUS PP2002 4-1

4. When adding a fill pattern to an object, you can add:
a. A textured fill
b. A picture fill
c. A semitransparent fill
d. All of the above
ANS: d
OBJ: 7-4
STO: MOUS PP2002 4-4

5. You use the Format Painter tool to:
a. Copy an object to another location
b. Copy the formatting from one object to another
c. Choose a border and/or fill for the selected object
d. All of the above
ANS: b
OBJ: 7-5
STO: MOUS PP2002 4-4

6. The icon on the Format Painter button displays:
a. A painter
b. Dots of various colors
c. A paintbrush
d. None of the above
ANS: c
OBJ: 7-5
STO: MOUS PP2002 4-4

7. Double-clicking the Format Painter button:
a. Deactivates the Format Painter and restores the normal mouse pointer
b. Does the same thing as a single-click
c. Does nothing because only single-clicks should be used
d. None of the above
ANS: d
OBJ: 7-5
STO: MOUS PP2002 4-4

8. You know that you have successfully selected a line when:
a. Four sizing handles appear
b. Two sizing handles appear
c. No sizing handles appear
d. A four-pointed arrow appears
ANS: b
OBJ: 7-1
STO: MOUS PP2002 4-1

9. A pre-mixed color is:
a. One that you created and saved by using the Custom Color dialog box
b. A color that you can choose from the Standard tab of the Color dialog box
c. A color designed to harmonize with your presentation's color scheme
d. A color that you create by dragging a crosshair on a color palette
ANS: b
OBJ: 7-3
STO: MOUS PP2002 4-4

10. Line weights can be:
a. Any thickness that you want
b. Any thickness but limited by the amount of memory available on your PC
c. From 1 to 3 points
d. From 1/4 to 6 points
ANS: a
OBJ: 7-1
STO: MOUS PP2002 4-1

11. To copy fill effects from one object to another, use the:
a. Copy command
b. Paste command
c. Format Painter
d. All of the above
ANS: c
OBJ: 7-5
STO: MOUS PP2002 4-4

12. Grayscale settings are sometimes used because:
   a. Grayscale is more trendsetting than color
   b. If you don't have a color printer, you can't otherwise print your presentation
   c. Fill colors might obscure text when printing in black-and-white
   d. Shades of gray are sometimes more dramatic than color

   ANS: c
   OBJ: 7-6
   STO: MOUS PP2002 4-5

13. You can apply gradient fills to:
   a. Lines
   b. Text boxes
   c. Arrowheads
   d. All of the above

   ANS: b
   OBJ: 7-2
   STO: MOUS PP2002 3-3

14. You can adjust the grayscale settings for:
   a. Text only
   b. A master slide
   c. Object fills only
   d. All of the above

   ANS: b
   OBJ: 7-6
   STO: MOUS PP2002 4-1

15. The following is a grayscale setting option:
   a. Light Grayscale
   b. Dark Grayscale
   c. Neutral Grayscale
   d. All of the above

   ANS: a
   OBJ: 7-6
   STO: MOUS PP2002 4-1

16. To create a very bright custom color, drag the crosshair:
   a. To the top of the color palette
   b. To the bottom of the color palette
   c. To the left side of the color palette
   d. To the right side of the color palette

   ANS: a
   OBJ: 7-3
   STO: MOUS PP2002 4-4

17. To apply a textured fill, open the Fill Effects dialog box and:
   a. Click the Gradient tab and choose one of the preset options
   b. Click the Pattern tab and then click the Options button
   c. Click the Texture tab
   d. None of the above

   ANS: d
   OBJ: 7-4
   STO: MOUS PP2002 4-4

18. If nothing appears when you key text in a selected AutoShape, the problem is most likely that:
   a. The text is the same color as the fill
   b. Your computer is malfunctioning and you need to reboot
   c. You forgot to choose a font style
   d. You chose a transparent text color

   ANS: a
   OBJ: 7-2
   STO: MOUS PP2002 3-3

19. When you use the Format Painter to copy a texture from an AutoShape to a text placeholder:
   a. The font formatting associated with the AutoShape, even when there's no text in the AutoShape, is applied to the text placeholder
   b. The font formatting associated with the AutoShape is applied to the text placeholder only when there is text in the AutoShape
   c. The Format Painter copies only fills and line formatting, never font formatting
   d. None of the above

   ANS: a
   OBJ: 7-5
   STO: MOUS PP2002 4-4

20. To copy formatting from an object on one slide to an object on a different slide:
   a. Use the Eye Dropper button
   b. Use the Copy Formatting and Paste Formatting commands on the shortcut menu
   c. Use the Format Painter button
   d. Copy the original object, paste it on the other slide, and then change its AutoShape

   ANS: c
   OBJ: 7-5
   STO: MOUS PP2002 4-4

Completion

1. An object will become invisible if it has no line color and ________________.
   ANS: No fill color
   OBJ: 7-2
   STO: MOUS PP2002 3-3

2. A fill effect that has one color blending into another is called a ________________.
   ANS: Gradient fill
   OBJ: 7-4
   STO: MOUS PP2002 4-4

3. If you use the Format Painter and have unanticipated results, you can choose the ________________ command to remedy the situation.
   ANS: Undo
   OBJ: 7-5
   STO: MOUS PP2002 4-4

4. You can copy formatting from one slide to another by using the ________________.
   ANS: Format Painter
   OBJ: 7-5
   STO: MOUS PP2002 4-4

5. After double-clicking the Format Painter feature, you can click the Format Painter tool again or press ________________ to turn it off.
   ANS: [Esc]
   OBJ: 7-5
   STO: MOUS PP2002 4-1

6. If you use the Format Painter to copy a fill effect from an AutoShape to a text box and you get an unexpected font, you can ________________ to restore the text box.
   ANS: Click Undo
   OBJ: 7-5
   STO: MOUS PP2002 4-4

7. If you want to use a fill color not shown when you click the Fill Color list box arrow, choose ________________.
   ANS: More Fill Colors
   OBJ: 7-2
   STO: MOUS PP2002 3-3

8. To apply a dashed line to the border of a text box, click the ________________ button on the Drawing toolbar.
   ANS: Dash Style
   OBJ: 7-1
   STO: MOUS PP2002 4-1

9. To apply identical grayscale settings to all text placeholders in a presentation, make the changes on the ________________.
ANS: Master slides
OBJ: 7-6
STO: MOUS PP2002 4-1

10. If the Picture toolbar is not displayed, you can choose Toolbars, Picture from the ________________ menu.
ANS: View
OBJ: 7-6
STO: MOUS PP2002 2-9

11. After drawing a square, you can right-click it and choose ________________ from the shortcut menu to change both the fill and border color.
ANS: Format AutoShape
OBJ: 7-1
STO: MOUS PP2002 4-1

12. You can change a solid line to a dotted line by clicking the ________________ button on the Drawing toolbar.
ANS: Line Style
OBJ: 7-1
STO: MOUS PP2002 4-1

13. To change an object's fill from a solid color to a pattern, click the ________________ button on the Drawing toolbar.
ANS: Fill Color
OBJ: 7-2
STO: MOUS PP2002 3-3

14. Early Sunset is an example of a ________________ gradient fill.
ANS: Preset
OBJ: 7-4
STO: MOUS PP2002 4-4

15. You can add a 6-pt border to an AutoShape by using the Format AutoShape dialog box or the ________________ button on the Drawing toolbar.
ANS: Line Style
OBJ: 7-1
STO: MOUS PP2002 4-1

16. When applying a gradient fill to a circle, use the ________________ shading style to make it appear like a globe or sphere.
ANS: From Center
OBJ: 7-4
STO: MOUS PP2002 4-4

17. If you applied a pattern to a text box, you can eliminate the pattern when you're printing the slide on a black-and-white printer by changing the grayscale settings for the text box to ________________.
ANS: White or Black with White Fill
OBJ: 7-6
STO: MOUS PP2002 4-1

18. To remove a border from a selected text box, choose ________________ in the Line Color button's list box.
ANS: No Line
OBJ: 7-2
STO: MOUS PP2002 3-3

19. If you key blue text in an AutoShape and then change the AutoShape's fill color to blue, the text will ________________.
ANS: Disappear
OBJ: 7-2
STO: MOUS PP2002 3-3

20. To access the transparency slider for a fill color, click ________________ on the Fill Color button's list box.
ANS: More Fill Colors
OBJ: 7-3
STO: MOUS PP2002 3-3

Lesson 8: Manipulating PowerPoint Objects

True/False

1. The Align Middle button on the Align or Distribute toolbar vertically aligns the center points of objects.
ANS: F
OBJ: 8-2
STO: MOUS PP2002 3-3

2. When you click the Relative to Slide button on the Align or Distribute toolbar, all alignment actions are relative to the slide, rather than to the selected objects.
ANS: T
OBJ: 8-2
STO: MOUS PP2002 3-3

3. You can use the ruler to help you position objects by choosing Ruler from the View menu.
ANS: T
OBJ: 8-2
STO: MOUS PP2002 3-3

4. After AutoShape objects are ungrouped, you can group them again by choosing Regroup from the Draw menu.
ANS: T
OBJ: 8-3
STO: MOUS PP2002 3-3

5. Object shadows and 3-D effects cannot be individually customized.
ANS: F
OBJ: 8-4
STO: MOUS PP2002 3-3

6. Shadows and 3-D effects should be used sparingly.
ANS: T
OBJ: 8-4
STO: MOUS PP2002 3-3

7. You can customize a 3-D effect on all types of objects, not just WordArt.
ANS: T
OBJ: 8-4
STO: MOUS PP2002 3-3

8. Duplicated objects cannot overlap one another.
ANS: F
OBJ: 8-5
STO: MOUS PP2002 3-3

9. The Duplicate command works only if the duplicate copy remains selected.
ANS: T
OBJ: 8-5
STO: MOUS PP2002 3-3

10. You can group all types of objects, including clip art and AutoShapes.
ANS: T
OBJ: 8-3
STO: MOUS PP2002 3-3

11. You can ungroup a vector-based clip art image by using the shortcut menu.
ANS: T
OBJ: 8-6
STO: MOUS PP2002 3-3

12. All clip art images can be ungrouped.
ANS: F
OBJ: 8-6
STO: MOUS PP2002 3-3

13. If you rotate multiple objects that are not grouped, the objects rotate independently.
ANS: T

OBJ: 8-2
STO: MOUS PP2002 3-3

14. Pressing [Ctrl]+[L] when the Slide pane is active selects all objects on the slide.
ANS: F
OBJ: 8-1
STO: MOUS PP2002 3-3

15. The Align or Distribute submenu can become a floating toolbar.
ANS: T
OBJ: 8-2
STO: MOUS PP2002 3-3

16. Gray selection handles indicate a selected object within a grouped collection of objects.
ANS: T
OBJ: 8-3
STO: MOUS PP2002 3-3

17. The Duplicate command enables you to place evenly spaced duplicates of a selected object in a horizontal, vertical, or diagonal row.
ANS: T
OBJ: 8-5
STO: MOUS PP2002 3-3

18. Object shadows can be changed to any color you want.
ANS: T
OBJ: 8-4
STO: MOUS PP2002 3-3

19. 3-D effects cannot be applied to text that is keyed in a text box.
ANS: T
OBJ: 8-4
STO: MOUS PP2002 3-3

20. After converting a clip art image to drawing objects, you can select and rotate just one object from the image.
ANS: T
OBJ: 8-3
STO: MOUS PP2002 3-3

Multiple Choice

1. To select all objects on a slide:
   a. Choose Select All from the Tools menu
   b. Press [Ctrl]+[A]
   c. Click the Select All button on the Formatting toolbar
   d. All of the above
   ANS: b
   OBJ: 8-1
   STO: MOUS PP2002 3-3

2. To select multiple objects:
   a. After selecting the first object, hold down Shift and select each desired additional object
   b. Choose Select All from the Tools menu
   c. Press [Ctrl]+[E]
   d. All of the above
   ANS: a
   OBJ: 8-1
   STO: MOUS PP2002 3-3

3. To deselect an object when a group of objects is selected:
   a. Click Undo
   b. Hold down [Alt] and click the object to deselect it
   c. Hold down [Shift] and click the object to deselect it
   d. Press [Esc]
   ANS: c
   OBJ: 8-1
   STO: MOUS PP2002 3-3

4. You can rotate or flip the following items on a slide:
   a. Text boxes
   b. WordArt
   c. Drawn objects
   d. All of the above
   ANS: d
   OBJ: 8-2
   STO: MOUS PP2002 3-3

5. The following indicates that objects have been grouped together:
   a. When you select them, there is only one set of sizing handles
   b. When you rotate them, they all rotate together
   c. Both a and b
   d. Neither a nor b
   ANS: c
   OBJ: 8-3
   STO: MOUS PP2002 3-3

6. Within a stack of objects, you can:
   a. Move an object to the top or bottom of the stack
   b. Move an object down one layer in the stack
   c. Bring an object up one layer in the stack
   d. All of the above
   ANS: d
   OBJ: 8-4
   STO: MOUS PP2002 3-3

7. To manipulate an object that is located behind several other objects, you can:
   a. Press [F7] until all objects are sent to the back and the desired object is on top
   b. Send the top objects to the back one at a time until the desired object is on top
   c. Press [Esc] until all objects are sent to the back and the desired object is on top
   d. All of the above
   ANS: b
   OBJ: 8-4
   STO: MOUS PP2002 3-3

8. You can use the shadow settings to:
   a. Change the angle of a shadow
   b. Change the shadow color
   c. Make a shadow semitransparent
   d. All of the above
   ANS: d
   OBJ: 8-4
   STO: MOUS PP2002 3-3

9. The purpose of the Duplicate command is to:
   a. Provide a shortcut for the Copy command
   b. Create evenly spaced duplicate objects in a straight line or at an angle
   c. Create evenly spaced duplicate arrows in a straight line or at an angle
   d. None of the above
   ANS: b
   OBJ: 8-5
   STO: MOUS PP2002 3-3

10. To duplicate a selected object:
    a. Choose Duplicate from the Edit menu
    b. Choose Duplicate from the Insert menu
    c. Click the Duplicate button on the Drawing toolbar
    d. None of the above
    ANS: a
    OBJ: 8-5
    STO: MOUS PP2002 3-3

11. A dialog box opens asking you if you want to convert an object to drawing objects when you:
    a. Ungroup a WordArt image

b. Ungroup a clip art image
c. Ungroup a freeform image
d. All of the above
ANS: b
OBJ: 8-6
STO: MOUS PP2002 3-3

12. To convert a vector image to drawing objects:
a. Click the Disassemble button on the Drawing toolbar
b. Click the Ungroup button on the Drawing toolbar
c. Choose Ungroup from the Draw menu
d. None of the above
ANS: c
OBJ: 8-6
STO: MOUS PP2002 3-3

13. If you convert a vector image to drawing objects, you can:
a. Delete part of the image
b. Change part of the image
c. Regroup the image
d. All of the above
ANS: d
OBJ: 8-6
STO: MOUS PP2002 3-3

14. After applying a 3-D effect to an object, you can use the 3-D Settings toolbar to change the:
a. 3-D color
b. Depth
c. Rotation angle
d. All of the above
ANS: d
OBJ: 8-4
STO: MOUS PP2002 3-3

15. When an object has gray selection handles, you can:
a. Change its size
b. Rotate it
c. Change its fill color
d. None of the above
ANS: c
OBJ: 8-6
STO: MOUS PP2002 3-3

16. If you have several objects selected and need to add one more object to the selection:
a. Hold down [Shift] and click the object
b. Hold down [Shift] and then press [Tab] one or more times
c. Hold down [Alt] and click the object
d. Any of the above
ANS: a
OBJ: 8-1
STO: MOUS PP2002 3-3

17. To select only one object when multiple objects are already selected:
a. Hold down [Ctrl] and click the object
b. Press [Tab] one or more times
c. Click the object without holding down [Ctrl] or [Shift] or [Alt]
d. b or c
ANS: d
OBJ: 8-1
STO: MOUS PP2002 3-3

18. When you draw a selection rectangle:
a. If the rectangle splits a text box, only the text inside the rectangle will be selected
b. Only objects that are completely contained inside the rectangle will be selected
c. All objects that the rectangle touches plus all objects inside the rectangle will be selected
d. Only the objects that the rectangle's border touches will be selected
ANS: b
OBJ: 8-1
STO: MOUS PP2002 3-3

19. To arrange a series of selected objects in a diagonal line from the upper-right corner to the lower-left corner of a slide:
a. Choose Align Diagonal Down from the Align or Distribute submenu
b. Display the ruler and then use it to help you place the objects by eye
c. Using the Align or Distribute menu, turn on the Relative to Slide option, click Align Top, click Align Right, click Distribute Horizontally, and then click Distribute Vertically
d. Open the Distribute dialog box, choose Distribute existing objects, and then choose Diagonal Down
ANS: c
OBJ: 8-2
STO: MOUS PP2002 3-3

20. To make an existing object shadow have more depth:
a. Change its color to black
b. Click appropriate Nudge buttons to move the shadow further away from the object
c. On the Shadow Settings toolbar, click the Color button, and choose Semitransparent from the Color button submenu
d. On the Shadow Settings toolbar, click the Depth button and choose a higher setting
ANS: b
OBJ: 8-4
STO: MOUS PP2002 3-3

Completion

1. When using your mouse pointer to select objects, you drag the mouse until you see a dotted box called a ____________________ surrounding the objects you want to select.
ANS: Selection rectangle
OBJ: 8-1
STO: MOUS PP2002 3-3

2. To display the Align or Distribute toolbar, click ____________________ on the Drawing toolbar and point to Align or Distribute.
ANS: Draw
OBJ: 8-2
STO: MOUS PP2002 3-3

3. ____________________ ensures that objects meant to stay together do not accidentally get moved individually or get deleted.
ANS: Grouping
OBJ: 8-3
STO: MOUS PP2002 3-3

4. You click the ____________________ button on the Order toolbar to send an object back one layer.
ANS: Send Backward
OBJ: 8-4
STO: MOUS PP2002 3-3

5. When applying object shadows and 3-D effects, you can choose from among ____________________ styles for each effect.
ANS: 20
OBJ: 8-4
STO: MOUS PP2002 3-3

6. You open the Shadow Settings toolbar by clicking the Shadow Style button on the ____________________ toolbar and choosing Shadow Settings.
ANS: Drawing
OBJ: 8-4
STO: MOUS PP2002 3-3

7. To duplicate an object, select it and press __________ __________ on the keyboard.
ANS: [Ctrl]+[D]
OBJ: 8-6
STO: MOUS PP2002 3-3

8. If you are using the Duplicate command and the duplicate copy is deselected, you must __________ __________.
ANS: Delete the copy and start over
OBJ: 8-5
STO: MOUS PP2002 3-3

9. When you __________ a clip art picture, you can manipulate its components as if they are AutoShapes or freeform objects.
ANS: Ungroup or Convert to drawing objects
OBJ: 8-6
STO: MOUS PP2002 3-3

10. To group objects, press __________ on the keyboard.
ANS: [Ctrl]+[Shift]+[G]
OBJ: 8-3
STO: MOUS PP2002 3-3

11. To ungroup objects, press __________ on the keyboard.
ANS: [Ctrl]+[Shift]+[H]
OBJ: 8-3
STO: MOUS PP2002 3-3

12. When you use the __________ command, a copy of the object you selected appears slightly offset from the original.
ANS: Duplicate
OBJ: 8-5
STO: MOUS PP2002 3-3

13. You can select all objects on a slide by choosing Select All from the __________ menu.
ANS: Edit
OBJ: 8-1
STO: MOUS PP2002 3-3

14. To vertically align the centers of objects, click the Align Center button on the __________ submenu.
ANS: Align or Distribute
OBJ: 8-2
STO: MOUS PP2002 3-3

15. To customize a shadow that has been applied to an object, select the object, click the Shadow Style button, and then select __________.
ANS: Shadow Settings
OBJ: 8-4
STO: MOUS PP2002 3-3

16. To convert a vector-based picture to drawing objects, choose __________ on the shortcut menu.
ANS: Grouping, Ungroup
OBJ: 8-7
STO: MOUS PP2002 3-3

17. To change an object to a horizontal mirror image of itself, choose __________ from the Draw menu.
ANS: Rotate or Flip, Flip Horizontal
OBJ: 8-2
STO: MOUS PP2002 3-3

18. To turn the ruler on or off, choose Ruler from the __________ menu.
ANS: View
OBJ: 8-2
STO: MOUS PP2002 3-3

19. To make a horizontal border of evenly spaced triangles from a single triangle that you drew, use the __________ command.
ANS: Duplicate
OBJ: 8-5
STO: MOUS PP2002 3-3

20. To space objects evenly in a horizontal line relative to each other use the __________ button on the Align or Distribute toolbar.
ANS: Distribute Horizontally
OBJ: 8-2
STO: MOUS PP2002 3-3

Lesson 9: Customizing Templates and Toolbars

True/False

1. If you right-click a toolbar, you can open a dialog box that will enable you to change the size of the toolbar buttons.
ANS: T
OBJ: 9-1
STO: MOUS PP2002 4-1

2. PowerPoint changes which toolbars are displayed depending on what you're doing. You cannot control which toolbars are displayed.
ANS: F
OBJ: 9-1
STO: MOUS PP2002 4-1

3. To create your own custom toolbar, click the New button on the Options tab of the Customize dialog box.
ANS: F
OBJ: 9-1
STO: MOUS PP2002 4-1

4. To change background effects for an entire presentation, you must first switch to a master slide.
ANS: F
OBJ: 9-2
STO: MOUS PP2002 3-2

5. Sometimes the master-slide graphics can interfere with the presentation slide designs.
ANS: T
OBJ: 9-2
STO: MOUS PP2002 3-2

6. The Background dialog box limits you to choosing only solid colors.
ANS: F
OBJ: 9-2
STO: MOUS PP2002 4-1

7. You can apply a template design from the Apply Design Template dialog box by choosing a presentation file with a .ppt extension.
ANS: T
OBJ: 9-5
STO: MOUS PP2002 1-1

8. You can save a presentation with special master-slide effects as a template for use with other presentations.
ANS: T
OBJ: 9-3
STO: MOUS PP2002 4-5

9. You use the Background dialog box only when you want to apply the same background to each slide in a presentation.

ANS: F
OBJ: 9-2
STO: MOUS PP2002 4-1

10. If you place a clip art image on the title master, it appears on each slide in your presentation.
ANS: F
OBJ: 9-3
STO: MOUS PP2002 4-5

11. You can have more than one design template in a single presentation.
ANS: T
OBJ: 9-5
STO: MOUS PP2002 4-1

12. Color schemes can be copied from one presentation to another.
ANS: T
OBJ: 9-5
STO: MOUS PP2002 4-5

13. You can copy and apply a design from one presentation to another presentation even if it is not saved as a template.
ANS: T
OBJ: 9-5
STO: MOUS PP2002 4-5

14. Backgrounds that you apply by using the Background dialog box can be solid colors, gradient fills, or bitmap images, but cannot be patterns.
ANS: F
OBJ: 9-2
STO: MOUS PP2002 3-2

15. Using the Background dialog box, you can change the background for an individual slide in a presentation.
ANS: T
OBJ: 9-2
STO: MOUS PP2002 4-1

16. To customize a presentation color scheme, right-click a color on the Fill Color button's list box and then choose a replacement color.
ANS: F
OBJ: 9-4
STO: MOUS PP2002 4-5

17. If an element on the slide master interferes with text on an individual slide, hide it by drawing a rectangle that matches the slide's background.
ANS: F
OBJ: 9-2
STO: MOUS PP2002 3-2

18. When you click Apply on the Background dialog box, another dialog box appears asking you which slide(s) to apply it to.
ANS: F
OBJ: 9-2
STO: MOUS PP2002 3-2

19. The Apply to All button applies an effect to all slides.
ANS: T
OBJ: 9-2
STO: MOUS PP2002 3-2

20. You can have more than one color scheme in a single presentation.
ANS: T
OBJ: 9-5
STO: MOUS PP2002 4-6

Multiple Choice

1. To add a button to a toolbar:
   a. Click the Command tab on the Customize dialog box, select a toolbar from the categories list, and then double-click an icon on the Commands list
   b. Choose a toolbar from the Toolbars tab in the Customize dialog box and then double-click an icon on the Commands tab
   c. Choose a category in the Commands tab of the Customize dialog box and then drag an icon onto the toolbar
   d. None of the above

   ANS: c
   OBJ: 9-1
   STO: MOUS PP2002 4-1

2. To create a new toolbar:
   a. Copy an existing toolbar, save it with a new name, and then remove the buttons you don't want and add new ones
   b. Open the Customize dialog box and then click the New button
   c. Open the Customize dialog box, scroll to the bottom of the list of toolbars, select the last entry that doesn't have a name yet, and key a name for it
   d. There is no way to make a new toolbar; you can only modify an existing one

   ANS: b
   OBJ: 9-1
   STO: MOUS PP2002 4-1

3. To remove a button from a toolbar:
   a. Open the Customize dialog box, click the Commands tab, and then drag the button off the toolbar
   b. Right-click the button on the toolbar and then choose Delete from the shortcut menu
   c. a or b
   d. None of the above

   ANS: a
   OBJ: 9-1
   STO: MOUS PP2002 4-1

4. Custom backgrounds can consist of:
   a. Gradient fills
   b. Textures
   c. Pictures
   d. All of the above

   ANS: d
   OBJ: 9-2
   STO: MOUS PP2002 4-4

5. To create your own design template from a presentation that you customized:
   a. Open the default template as a template (not a presentation) and use the Format Painter to copy the design to it
   b. Delete all the slides, leaving just the slide and title masters, and then, using the Save As command, change the Save As Type to Design Template
   c. Open the design template your presentation was based on, duplicate all the changes you made to the slide master and title master, and then save the template with a new name
   d. You cannot create your own templates

   ANS: b
   OBJ: 9-3
   STO: MOUS PP2002 4-5

6. After you create a custom color scheme, if you add it as a standard scheme:
   a. It is available to any presentation that you create in the future
   b. It is available to any presentation that you create based on the current design template
   c. It is available only to the presentation that you are currently working on or copies you make of that presentation

d. It is available only if you create a design template based on the current presentation
ANS: c
OBJ: 9-4
STO: MOUS PP2002 4-5

7. When copying a color scheme between presentations:
a. You can be in any view
b. Change to Slide Master view
c. Change to Slide Show view
d. None of the above
ANS: b
OBJ: 9-5
STO: MOUS PP2002 4-5

8. To save a custom design that you created as a design template:
a. Use the Save As Type list box on the Save As dialog box
b. Use the Save As Template command on the File menu
c. Choose Design Template from the File Name list box on the Save As dialog box
d. Any of the above
ANS: a
OBJ: 9-3
STO: MOUS PP2002 4-5

9. To customize a color scheme:
a. You must be working on the default design template
b. You must change the background color before you can change any other color
c. Click Edit Color Schemes below the color scheme thumbnails on the Slide Design task pane
d. All of the above
ANS: c
OBJ: 9-4
STO: MOUS PP2002 4-5

10. To make a text box with a gradient fill appear on each slide in a presentation:
a. Place it on the title master
b. Place it on the slide master
c. a and b
d. None of the above, because objects with gradient fills must be copied individually to each slide in the presentation
ANS: c
OBJ: 9-3
STO: MOUS PP2002 4-5

11. To copy a presentation design from one presentation to an individual slide on another presentation, use the Format Painter button to:
a. Copy a slide thumbnail's formatting from one presentation to another's slide thumbnail
b. Copy a slide master thumbnail's formatting from one presentation to another's slide master thumbnail
c. Copy a slide master thumbnail's formatting from one presentation to a slide thumbnail on the other presentation
d. None of the above, because you must use a design template to apply a slide design
ANS: a
OBJ: 9-5
STO: MOUS PP2002 4-6

12. To copy a presentation's color scheme from one presentation to another, use the Format Painter button to:
a. Copy a slide thumbnail's formatting from one presentation to another's slide thumbnail
b. Copy a slide master thumbnail's formatting from one presentation to another's slide master thumbnail
c. Copy a slide master thumbnail's formatting from one presentation to a slide thumbnail on the other presentation
d. None of the above, because you must apply a design template to get a different color scheme
ANS: b
OBJ: 9-5
STO: MOUS PP2002 4-5

13. You can save a presentation that you created as a new design template:
a. Only in PowerPoint's template folder
b. Only in PowerPoint's template folder or in a folder formatted specifically for PowerPoint design templates
c. In any folder that you like
d. Only in PowerPoint's template folder or on a floppy disk
ANS: c
OBJ: 9-3
STO: MOUS PP2002 4-5

14. The number of design templates that you can have in a single presentation:
a. Is limited to one-third of the number of slides in the presentation
b. Is unlimited, but they must all use the same color scheme
c. Is limited to three separate designs
d. Is limited only by your sense of artistic style
ANS: d
OBJ: 9-5
STO: MOUS PP2002 4-6

15. When you choose colors for a customized color scheme:
a. You are limited to the colors shown on the standard colors honeycomb
b. You can use custom colors that you mix by using the color palette
c. You are limited to three color changes in a given color scheme
d. You can change any of the colors except the two colors used for hyperlinks
ANS: b
OBJ: 9-4
STO: MOUS PP2002 4-5

16. To apply a design template that is saved on a floppy disk:
a. First copy the template to PowerPoint's template folder
b. Open the My Computer or Windows Explorer window, and then open the floppy drive folder and double-click the template file
c. Click the Browse button below the design template thumbnails in the Slide Design task pane, navigate to your floppy drive, and then double-click the template file
d. Either b or c
ANS: c
OBJ: 9-3
STO: MOUS PP2002 1-1

17. If you want a picture image to appear as a background on all slides in a presentation, you can:
a. Insert a picture on the slide master, size it to fit the entire slide, and send it to the back
b. Open the Background dialog box, choose Fill Effects, and then click the Textures tab
c. Click the Insert menu and then choose Picture, Background
d. None of the above
ANS: a
OBJ: 9-2
STO: MOUS PP2002 3-2

18. You can use transparency settings to create added interest on:
    a. Any background effect
    b. Backgrounds that use textures
    c. Backgrounds that use gradient fills
    d. None of the above
    ANS: d
    OBJ: 9-2
    STO: MOUS PP2002 3-2
19. A color scheme consists of:
    a. Eight colors
    b. Eight standard colors plus two hyperlink colors
    c. Ten colors
    d. As many colors as you need
    ANS: a
    OBJ: 9-4
    STO: MOUS PP2002 4-5
20. Using the Background dialog box, you can place the following on a slide:
    a. Placeholder
    b. Bitmap image
    c. WordArt image
    d. Any of the above
    ANS: b
    OBJ: 9-2
    STO: MOUS PP2002 4-1

Completion

1. To add a button to a toolbar, ________________ it from the Commands list in the Customize dialog box.
   ANS: Drag
   OBJ: 9-1
   STO: MOUS PP2002 4-1
2. When you create a new toolbar, you must ________ ________ in the New Toolbar dialog box.
   ANS: Name it or Key a name
   OBJ: 9-1
   STO: MOUS PP2002 4-1
3. If you want to delete a custom toolbar, open the Customize dialog box, and then ______________ ______________________.
   ANS: Select the toolbar and click the Delete button
   OBJ: 9-1
   STO: MOUS PP2002 4-1
4. To remove a button from a custom toolbar, _______ ___________________.
   ANS: Drag it off the toolbar
   OBJ: 9-1
   STO: MOUS PP2002 4-1
5. You can use the ________________ dialog box to eliminate master-slide graphics on individual slides.
   ANS: Background
   OBJ: 9-2
   STO: MOUS PP2002 3-2
6. If the graphic elements on the slide master interfere with one of the slides in your presentation, you can choose to omit the background graphics in the ________________ dialog box.
   ANS: Background
   OBJ: 9-2
   STO: MOUS PP2002 3-2
7. To apply a texture to a background, choose ______ ___________ after clicking the Background Fill list box option.
   ANS: Fill Effects
   OBJ: 9-3
   STO: MOUS PP2002 3-2
8. You must place all graphics and formatting on the ________________ if you want them to be included in a template that you are designing.
   ANS: Master slides
   OBJ: 9-3
   STO: MOUS PP2002 4-5
9. The Color Scheme dialog box contains the Standard tab and the ________________ tab.
   ANS: Custom
   OBJ: 9-4
   STO: MOUS PP2002 4-5
10. If you want to customize a color scheme for just one slide in your presentation, you must __________ ____________________ before opening the Edit Color Scheme dialog box.
    ANS: Select the slide's thumbnail
    OBJ: 9-4
    STO: MOUS PP2002 4-5
11. To keep background graphics placed on a slide master from appearing on the current slide, select the ______________________________ option in the Background dialog box.
    ANS: Omit Background Graphics from Master
    OBJ: 9-2
    STO: MOUS PP2002 2-3
12. To copy a color scheme from one presentation to another, use the Format Painter to click _________ ______________.
    ANS: A master thumbnail or A slide master thumbnail
    OBJ: 9-5
    STO: MOUS PP2002 4-5
13. To save a presentation as a design template, open the Save As dialog box and then choose Design Template from the ________________ list box.
    ANS: Save As Type
    OBJ: 9-3
    STO: MOUS PP2002 4-5
14. When using a picture fill for a slide background, you can preserve the picture's proportions if you select the ________________________ option on the Picture tab.
    ANS: Lock Picture Aspect Ratio
    OBJ: 9-2
    STO: MOUS PP2002 4-1
15. To create a template from a plain white slide, start a new presentation using the ________________ template.
    ANS: Default design
    OBJ: 9-3
    STO: MOUS PP2002 4-5
16. You can ungroup a clip art image if it is a ________ ________ image and not a bitmap image.
    ANS: Vector
    OBJ: 9-3
    STO: MOUS PP2002 4-5
17. Use the ________________ button on the Standard toolbar to copy a design template from one presentation to another.
    ANS: Format Painter
    OBJ: 9-5
    STO: MOUS PP2002 4-5
18. To copy a color scheme from one presentation to another, you must have ________________ view displayed.
    ANS: Slide Master
    OBJ: 9-5
    STO: MOUS PP2002 4-5

19. One way to choose a different design template for your presentation is to __________________ the current template's name on the status bar.
ANS: Double-click
OBJ: 9-3
STO: MOUS PP2002 1-1

20. If the design template you want is not displayed as a thumbnail in the Slide Design task pane, click __________________ at the bottom of the screen to open the Apply Design Template dialog box.
ANS: Browse
OBJ: 9-3
STO: MOUS PP2002 1-1

Lesson 10: Advanced Text Manipulation

True/False

1. To create different indents for different paragraphs, you must put them in separate text boxes.
ANS: T
OBJ: 10-1
STO: MOUS PP2002 2-2

2. When a text box is active, if the ruler is displayed, it indicates the width of the text box.
ANS: T
OBJ: 10-1
STO: MOUS PP2002 2-2

3. To change indents on the ruler, it is not necessary to place the insertion point inside a text box.
ANS: F
OBJ: 10-1
STO: MOUS PP2002 2-2

4. You can change the distance between bullets and text in a text placeholder.
ANS: T
OBJ: 10-1
STO: MOUS PP2002 2-2

5. Indent settings that you apply to individual slides before you change the slide-master placeholder indents are not changed until you reapply the slide layout.
ANS: T
OBJ: 10-1
STO: MOUS PP2002 2-2

6. After you set tabs for columns in a table, the settings cannot be changed.
ANS: F
OBJ: 10-2
STO: MOUS PP2002 2-2

7. Increasing the zoom setting enlarges both the slide and the ruler.
ANS: T
OBJ: 10-2
STO: MOUS PP2002 2-2

8. Line spacing within paragraphs can be changed in increments of only one line.
ANS: F
OBJ: 10-3
STO: MOUS PP2002 2-2

9. The default setting for line spacing within paragraphs is measured in points.
ANS: F
OBJ: 10-3
STO: MOUS PP2002 2-2

10. You can change paragraph spacing as well as line spacing.
ANS: T
OBJ: 10-3
STO: MOUS PP2002 2-2

11. Changing the page size setting can distort the graphics in a presentation.
ANS: T
OBJ: 10-5
STO: MOUS PP2002 4-1

12. The default page orientation setting for slides is Portrait.
ANS: F
OBJ: 10-5
STO: MOUS PP2002 4-1

13. Hanging indents are used mainly for bulleted text.
ANS: T
OBJ: 10-1
STO: MOUS PP2002 2-2

14. When working with text-box settings, you can make text wrap to fit the width of an object or you can make an object resize itself to the size of its text.
ANS: T
OBJ: 10-4
STO: MOUS PP2002 3-3

15. When you choose a Bottom Centered anchor point for a text box, decreasing the height of the text box will remove any extra space not used by text at the top of the text box.
ANS: T
OBJ: 10-4
STO: MOUS PP2002 3-3

16. You can change left and right margins in a text box, but not the top and bottom margins.
ANS: F
OBJ: 10-4
STO: MOUS PP2002 2-2

17. Working on a handout master, you can add, delete, or change the size of slide placeholders.
ANS: F
OBJ: 10-6
STO: MOUS PP2002 1-3

18. It is always best to decide on slide size and orientation before starting to create a presentation.
ANS: T
OBJ: 10-5
STO: MOUS PP2002 4-1

19. An indication that the word wrap and resize to fit options are turned off is that text remains on one line and expands beyond the edges of the AutoShape in which it is keyed.
ANS: T
OBJ: 10-4
STO: MOUS PP2002 3-3

20. An indication that resize to fit is turned on and word wrap is turned off is that an AutoShape keeps getting wider as you key text.
ANS: T
OBJ: 10-4
STO: MOUS PP2002 3-3

Multiple Choice

1. The top triangle on the ruler of a selected text box indicates:
a. The first-line indent marker
b. The last-line indent marker
c. The left indent marker
d. None of the above

ANS: a
OBJ: 10-1
STO: MOUS PP2002 2-2

2. The bottom triangle on the ruler of a selected text box indicates:
   a. The first-line indent marker
   b. The last-line indent marker
   c. The left indent marker
   d. None of the above
   ANS: c
   OBJ: 10-1
   STO: MOUS PP2002 2-2
3. To move both the top and bottom triangles on the ruler at the same time:
   a. Select the triangles and drag them in the direction you want to go
   b. Hold down Shift and drag them in the direction you want to go
   c. Select the small rectangle and drag it in the direction you want to go
   d. None of the above
   ANS: c
   OBJ: 10-1
   STO: MOUS PP2002 2-2
4. A hanging indent aligns:
   a. Text evenly on the left
   b. Text evenly on the right
   c. The first line to the right of the remaining lines
   d. The first line to the left of the remaining lines
   ANS: d
   OBJ: 10-1
   STO: MOUS PP2002 2-2
5. A first line indent aligns:
   a. Text evenly on the left
   b. Text evenly on the right
   c. The first line to the right of the remaining lines
   d. The first line to the left of the remaining lines
   ANS: c
   OBJ: 10-1
   STO: MOUS PP2002 2-2
6. To remove a tab marker:
   a. Select the tab and press [Delete]
   b. Select the tab and choose Cut from the Edit menu
   c. Drag the tab off the ruler
   d. All of the above
   ANS: c
   OBJ: 10-2
   STO: MOUS PP2002 2-2
7. Tab and indent settings affect the following text in a placeholder:
   a. Selected text only
   b. All text except the column headings
   c. Column headings only
   d. All text
   ANS: d
   OBJ: 10-1, 10-2
   STO: MOUS PP2002 2-2
8. To change line spacing between lines within a paragraph:
   a. Line spacing cannot be changed
   b. Choose Line Spacing from the Format menu
   c. Choose Line Spacing from the Edit menu
   d. None of the above
   ANS: b
   OBJ: 10-3
   STO: MOUS PP2002 2-2
9. To change spacing between paragraphs:
   a. You can change only the spacing after a paragraph
   b. You can change only the spacing before a paragraph
   c. You can change the spacing after or before a paragraph
   d. You cannot change spacing between paragraphs
   ANS: c
   OBJ: 10-3
   STO: MOUS PP2002 2-2
10. When you key text in an AutoShape, text is automatically formatted as follows:
    a. It is anchored at the middle, center position
    b. Word wrap is turned off
    c. Resize AutoShape is turned off
    d. All of the above
    ANS: d
    OBJ: 10-4
    STO: MOUS PP2002 3-3
11. To increase paragraph spacing:
    a. Click the Increase Paragraph button on the Standard toolbar
    b. Choose Line Spacing from the Format menu
    c. Choose Line Spacing from the Edit menu
    d. None of the above
    ANS: b
    OBJ: 10-3
    STO: MOUS PP2002 2-2
12. You can change the text anchor point to:
    a. Top Centered
    b. Bottom Centered
    c. Middle Centered
    d. Any of the above
    ANS: d
    OBJ: 10-4
    STO: MOUS PP2002 3-3
13. You can display and print presentations:
    a. As overhead transparencies
    b. As 35mm slides
    c. As black-and-white printouts
    d. All of the above
    ANS: d
    OBJ: 10-5
    STO: MOUS PP2002 4-1
14. The default page setup orientation is Portrait for:
    a. Slides
    b. Handouts
    c. Notes
    d. b and c
    ANS: d
    OBJ: 10-5
    STO: MOUS PP2002 4-1
15. The following placeholders can be changed on a handout master:
    a. Slide
    b. Date
    c. Filename
    d. All of the above
    ANS: b
    OBJ: 10-6
    STO: MOUS PP2002 1-3
16. The following output settings can be changed in the Page Setup dialog box:
    a. Width of the slide
    b. Number of slides to print
    c. Outline orientation
    d. a and c
    ANS: d
    OBJ: 10-5
    STO: MOUS PP2002 4-1

17. If you key text in an AutoShape and it spills over the shape's edges, you can fix the problem most easily by:
    a. Drawing a new larger AutoShape, copying the text to the new shape, and deleting the old one
    b. Turning off word wrap
    c. Turning on Resize AutoShape to Fit Text
    d. Turning off AutoMargins
    ANS: c
    OBJ: 10-4
    STO: MOUS PP2002 3-3
18. To change the margins in an AutoShape:
    a. Drag the yellow diamond-shaped handle, if it is available
    b. Choose AutoMargins from the shortcut menu
    c. Key margin measurements on the Text Box tab of the Format AutoShape dialog box
    d. b or c
    ANS: c
    OBJ: 10-4
    STO: MOUS PP2002 2-2
19. You can do the following to text in an AutoShape:
    a. Rotate the text within the AutoShape by 15-degree increments
    b. Eliminate its anchor point
    c. Increase its right margin
    d. All of the above
    ANS: c
    OBJ: 10-4
    STO: MOUS PP2002 2-2
20. To wrap text in a floating text box without using the Format Text Box dialog box:
    a. Choose Word Wrap from the Formatting menu
    b. Choose Word Wrap from the Tools menu
    c. Make the text box narrower by dragging one of its sizing handles
    d. None of the above
    ANS: c
    OBJ: 10-4
    STO: MOUS PP2002 2-2

Completion

1. The default tab setting is left-aligned at ___________________-inch intervals.
   ANS: 1
   OBJ: 10-2
   STO: MOUS PP2002 2-2
2. The number of tab-alignment types available in PowerPoint is __________________.
   ANS: 4
   OBJ: 10-2
   STO: MOUS PP2002 2-2
3. A __________________ tab is often used when working with numbers.
   ANS: Decimal
   OBJ: 10-2
   STO: MOUS PP2002 2-2
4. To align column headings in a tabbed table, sometimes you need to place them in a separate __________________.
   ANS: Text box
   OBJ: 10-2
   STO: MOUS PP2002 2-2
5. Each time you click the Tab Type button, a different icon appears, indicating the type of __________________.
   ANS: Tab alignment
   OBJ: 10-2
   STO: MOUS PP2002 2-2
6. Line spacing can be set in points or __________________ units.
   ANS: Line
   OBJ: 10-3
   STO: MOUS PP2002 2-2
7. To increase line spacing within a paragraph, choose Line Spacing on the __________________ menu.
   ANS: Formatting
   OBJ: 10-3
   STO: MOUS PP2002 2-2
8. You can change the position of text within a text box or AutoShape by using the Text Box tab in the __________________ dialog box.
   ANS: Format AutoShape or Format Text Box
   OBJ: 10-4
   STO: MOUS PP2002 3-3
9. When you choose the __________________ option, the text box automatically shrinks or grows as you add or delete text.
   ANS: Resize AutoShape to Fit Text
   OBJ: 10-4
   STO: MOUS PP2002 3-3
10. The text __________________ specifies the position where text begins in an object.
    ANS: Anchor point
    OBJ: 10-4
    STO: MOUS PP2002 3-3
11. You can use __________________settings to change the space between the text and the edge of a text box.
    ANS: Internal margin
    OBJ: 10-4
    STO: MOUS PP2002 2-2
12. To open the Page Setup dialog box, choose Page Setup from the __________________ menu.
    ANS: File
    OBJ: 10-5
    STO: MOUS PP2002 4-1
13. The first button on the Handout Master toolbar shows how handouts will print with __________________ slide(s) on the page.
    ANS: 1
    OBJ: 10-6
    STO: MOUS PP2002 1-3
14. You cannot alter the position of __________________ on the handout master.
    ANS: Slides
    OBJ: 10-6
    STO: MOUS PP2002 1-3
15. To make a multi-line text block left aligned, but centered within an AutoShape, change the __________________ setting to Middle Centered.
    ANS: Text anchor point
    OBJ: 10-4
    STO: MOUS PP2002 3-3
16. If you apply a contrasting outline color to a text box, you can provide space between the border and the text by changing the __________________ settings on the Text Box tab of the Format AutoShape dialog box.
    ANS: Internal margin
    OBJ: 10-4
    STO: MOUS PP2002 2-2
17. If you want a tabular column of numbers to be aligned by their decimal points, place a decimal-aligned tab marker on the __________________.
    ANS: Ruler
    OBJ: 10-2
    STO: MOUS PP2002 2-2

Question Bank

18. You can move text further away from its bullet without changing the bullet position by dragging the ____________________.
ANS: Left indent marker
OBJ: 10-1
STO: MOUS PP2002 2-2

19. You can move a bullet closer to its text without changing the text position by dragging the ____________________.
ANS: First-line indent marker
OBJ: 10-1
STO: MOUS PP2002 2-2

20. You can simultaneously move both a bullet and its text to the right by dragging ____________________ on the ruler.
ANS: The small rectangle (square)
OBJ: 10-1
STO: MOUS PP2002 2-2

Lesson 11: Animation and Slide Show Effects

True/False

1. Creating a summary slide generates a bulleted list from the titles of the selected slides, automatically inserting the new slide at the end of the selected slides.
ANS: F
OBJ: 11-7
STO: MOUS PP2002 4-10

2. You can use summary slides to provide either an introduction at the beginning of the presentation or a wrap-up at the end.
ANS: T
OBJ: 11-7
STO: MOUS PP2002 4-10

3. Creating a custom show means adding animations and slide transitions to a presentation.
ANS: F
OBJ: 11-7
STO: MOUS PP2002 7-1

4. Too many special effects can make it more difficult for the viewer to focus on the message of the presentation.
ANS: T
OBJ: 11-1
STO: MOUS PP2002 4-2

5. You cannot choose Hide Slide from the shortcut menu.
ANS: F
OBJ: 11-6
STO: MOUS PP2002 7-1

6. Hidden slides appear in Normal view.
ANS: T
OBJ: 11-6
STO: MOUS PP2002 6-2

7. Object animations can include sound effects.
ANS: T
OBJ: 11-5
STO: MOUS PP2002 6-2

8. You can apply as many animation effects as you want to a single object.
ANS: T
OBJ: 11-1
STO: MOUS PP2002 4-2

9. When you copy an animated object to another slide or another presentation, the animations are copied along with the object.
ANS: T
OBJ: 11-4
STO: MOUS PP2002 4-2

10. You cannot apply animation effects to elements in a design template.
ANS: F
OBJ: 11-3
STO: MOUS PP2002 4-2

11. You can float the Action Buttons submenu.
ANS: T
OBJ: 11-7
STO: MOUS PP2002 4-10

12. Hyperlinks are useful for presentations containing summary slides.
ANS: T
OBJ: 11-7
STO: MOUS PP2002 4-10

13. You set slide timings for presentations in which slides are advanced manually.
ANS: F
OBJ: 11-6
STO: MOUS PP2002 4-7

14. An agenda slide is a variation of a summary slide.
ANS: T
OBJ: 11-7
STO: MOUS PP2002 4-10

15. A sound object can be hidden by moving it off the slide into the gray area.
ANS: T
OBJ: 11-5
STO: MOUS PP2002 6-2

16. You can see a preview of a selected movie in the Insert Clip Art task pane.
ANS: T
OBJ: 11-4
STO: MOUS PP2002 6-2

17. You can change the size of an animated clip art image.
ANS: T
OBJ: 11-5
STO: MOUS PP2002 6-2

18. You can create a hyperlink on any slide in your presentation that links to another presentation.
ANS: T
OBJ: 11-7
STO: MOUS PP2002 4-10

19. You can create a hyperlink on any slide in your presentation that links to an Internet Web site.
ANS: T
OBJ: 11-7
STO: MOUS PP2002 4-10

20. When you insert a sound clip, the blue speaker icon appears only if you choose not to have the sound play automatically.
ANS: F
OBJ: 11-5
STO: MOUS PP2002 6-2

Multiple Choice

1. Creating a summary slide means making:
   a. A new slide containing the titles of selected slides
   b. A series of slides summarizing selected items in the outline

c. A series of slides summarizing all items in the outline
d. None of the above
ANS: a
OBJ: 11-7
STO: MOUS PP2002 4-10

2. Summary slides are created from
a. First-level bullets
b. Speaker notes
c. Slide titles
d. Header and footer text
ANS: c
OBJ: 11-7
STO: MOUS PP2002 4-10

3. Slides can be hidden to:
a. Create a short presentation from a longer one
b. Hide sensitive information
c. Hide optional information
d. All of the above
ANS: d
OBJ: 11-6
STO: MOUS PP2002 7-1

4. A summary slide:
a. Contains the text from the Notes pane for each slide in a presentation
b. Is generally used to list the presenter's credentials and cite reference material
c. Is created from the titles of selected slides
d. Lists the names of custom shows that are part of the presentation
ANS: c
OBJ: 11-7
STO: MOUS PP2002 4-10

5. You can animate the following objects:
a. A table
b. WordArt
c. Clip art
d. All of the above
ANS: d
OBJ: 11-1
STO: MOUS PP2002 4-2

6. A hyperlink object can be:
a. A button
b. Special text
c. A clip art image or an object that you draw
d. All of the above
ANS: d
OBJ: 11-7
STO: MOUS PP2002 4-10

7. You can create a hyperlink in a PowerPoint presentation that links to:
a. Another PowerPoint presentation
b. The Internet
c. An Excel file
d. All of the above
ANS: d
OBJ: 11-6
STO: MOUS PP2002 4-10

8. When you click the Forward or Next button on the Action Buttons submenu, the pointer changes to:
a. An I-beam
b. A cross
c. A two-pointed arrow
d. None of the above
ANS: b
OBJ: 11-7
STO: MOUS PP2002 4-10

9. PowerPoint's Rehearse Timings command enables you to:
a. Control the amount of time that a slide is displayed before automatically advancing to the next slide
b. Change the speed at which an automatic animation occurs
c. Control the amount of time between successive automatic animations on a slide
d. Edit speaker notes if they are too short or too long
ANS: a
OBJ: 11-6
STO: MOUS PP2002 4-7

10. The Set Up Show dialog box enables you to:
a. Temporarily change the color scheme for a presentation
b. List two or more presentations to be shown automatically, one after the other
c. Change from advancing slides automatically to advancing them manually
d. Record a narration for slide shows that run automatically
ANS: c
OBJ: 11-8
STO: MOUS PP2002 7-1

11. To change the order of animations on a slide:
a. Double-click the gray animation tag next to an object on the slide and change its number
b. Drag an item in the custom animation list up or down
c. Increase or decrease the delay time for an animated tem
d. Use the Order commands (bring forward, send to back, etc.)
ANS: b
OBJ: 11-4
STO: MOUS PP2002 4-2

12. To open the Custom Animation task pane:
a. Choose Custom Animation from the Slide Show menu
b. Click Custom Animation in the Slide Sorter toolbar
c. Press [Ctrl]+[A]
d. All of the above
ANS: a
OBJ: 11-1
STO: MOUS PP2002 4-2

13. You put an action button on a slide when you want to:
a. Provide a way to quickly return to a summary slide
b. Provide a way to display the Notes pane during a slide show
c. Provide a button to click when you want to use the annotation pen
d. All of the above
ANS: a
OBJ: 11-7
STO: MOUS PP2002 4-10

14. Besides using one of the buttons on the Action Buttons submenu, you can create an action button from:
a. A clip art image
b. A sound object
c. A slide thumbnail
d. a and b
ANS: a
OBJ: 11-7
STO: MOUS PP2002 4-5

15. To remove an animation:
a. Select the animated object, delete it, and then re-create it without the animation
b. Select the gray animation tag associated with the animated object and press [Delete] on your keyboard

c. Right-click the gray animation tag associated with the animated object and then choose Remove Animation from the shortcut menu
d. Right-click the item in the custom animation list and then choose Remove from the shortcut menu

ANS: d
OBJ: 11-1
STO: MOUS PP2002 4-2

16. If you insert a sound clip but don't want the blue loudspeaker icon to show on your slide, you can:
    a. Choose the play automatically option when inserting the sound clip
    b. Change the fill color of the loudspeaker icon to No Fill
    c. Drag the loudspeaker icon to a location off the slide
    d. Place another object on top of the sound icon

    ANS: c
    OBJ: 11-5
    STO: MOUS PP2002 6-2

17. To insert a link to another PowerPoint presentation:
    a. Choose the Presentation command on the Insert menu
    b. Choose the Hyperlink command on the Insert menu
    c. Click the PowerPoint Presentation button on the Action Buttons submenu
    d. Choose the File command on the Insert menu

    ANS: b
    OBJ: 11-7
    STO: MOUS PP2002 4-10

18. To insert a video clip or movie into your presentation:
    a. From the Insert menu, choose Movies and Sounds, Sound from Clip Organizer
    b. From the Slide Show menu, choose Custom Animation, Sound from Clip Organizer
    c. From the Slide Show menu, choose Animation Schemes, Sound from Clip Organizer
    d. Any of the above

    ANS: a
    OBJ: 11-5
    STO: MOUS PP2002 6-2

19. An agenda slide can:
    a. List the topics to be discussed
    b. Contain links to the first slide for each topic in the presentation
    c. Use Custom Shows to divide a presentation into logical parts
    d. All of the above

    ANS: d
    OBJ: 11-7
    STO: MOUS PP2002 4-10

20. As used in PowerPoint, a movie refers to:
    a. An object that moves along a motion path
    b. An object that has a delayed appearance on a slide
    c. An animated clip art image
    d. A text animation scheme

    ANS: c
    OBJ: 11-5
    STO: MOUS PP2002 6-2

Completion

1. To create a new slide from titles of selected slides, click the ________________ button on the Outlining toolbar.
   ANS: Summary Slide
   OBJ: 11-7
   STO: MOUS PP2002 4-10

2. The Summary Slide button is on the ________________ toolbar.
   ANS: Outlining or Slide Sorter
   OBJ: 11-7
   STO: MOUS PP2002 4-10

3. The shortcut menu containing the Hide Slide command will appear if you right-click ________________.
   ANS: A slide thumbnail
   OBJ: 11-7
   STO: MOUS PP2002 7-1

4. You can ________________ objects on a slide by adding special visual or sound effects to them.
   ANS: Animate
   OBJ: 11-1
   STO: MOUS PP2002 4-2

5. If you want an object that is on a slide to do something after it appears on a slide, for example, spin, apply a(n) ________________ effect to the object.
   ANS: Emphasis
   OBJ: 11-1
   STO: MOUS PP2002 4-2

6. The small gray numbered box that appears on a slide next to an animated object is called a(n) ________________.
   ANS: Animation tag
   OBJ: 11-1
   STO: MOUS PP2002 4-2

7. Underlined text that when clicked with the mouse jumps to a new slide is called a ________________.
   ANS: Hyperlink
   OBJ: 11-7
   STO: MOUS PP2002 4-10

8. If you set automatic slide timings and your slides do not advance automatically during a slide show, you need to change the Advance Slides setting in the ________________ dialog box.
   ANS: Set Up Show
   OBJ: 11-8
   STO: MOUS PP2002 7-1

9. You use the ________________ dialog box to set transitions between slides.
   ANS: Slide Transition
   OBJ: 11-1
   STO: MOUS PP2002 5-4

10. You can ________________ slides that contain optional or sensitive information so they do not appear during a slide show.
    ANS: Hide
    OBJ: 11-7
    STO: MOUS PP2002 7-1

11. Hidden slides do not appear in ________________ view.
    ANS: Slide Show
    OBJ: 11-6
    STO: MOUS PP2002 7-1

12. If you want an object to appear on a slide after the slide is displayed, apply a(n) ________________ effect to the object.
    ANS: Entrance
    OBJ: 11-1
    STO: MOUS PP2002 4-2

13. To add a text animation to all body text in a presentation, apply the animation to ________________.
    ANS: The body text placeholder on the slide master
    OBJ: 11-3
    STO: MOUS PP2002 4-2

14. To make a sound play each time a slide changes, insert a sound clip on ______________________.
ANS: The slide master
OBJ: 11-5
STO: MOUS PP2002 6-2

15. Automatic slide timings are intended for use with kiosks and other times when a speaker will not be used. Slide timings do not work well with ________ ________.
ANS: Action buttons or Hyperlinks
OBJ: 11-6
STO: MOUS PP2002 4-7

16. When you want to use hyperlinks during a presentation, be sure to turn off the Advance Slides Using Timings setting in the ________________ dialog box.
ANS: Set Up Show
OBJ: 11-6
STO: MOUS PP2002 7-1

17. An animation effect that controls how an animated object disappears or leaves the slide is called a(n) ________________ effect.
ANS: Exit
OBJ: 11-1
STO: MOUS PP2002 4-2

18. If you want to add a link to a summary or agenda slide, or links to the next and previous slides, you can use the ________________ command on the Slide Show menu.
ANS: Action Buttons
OBJ: 11-7
STO: MOUS PP2002 4-10

19. The easiest way to give each slide in your presentation the ability to jump back to an agenda slide is to ______________________________________ ______________________________.
ANS: Create a Home button on the slide master that links to the agenda slide
OBJ: 11-7
STO: MOUS PP2002 4-10

20. To make a sound clip play repeatedly until you press Esc, right-click its icon and choose ______________ ________ from the shortcut menu.
ANS: Edit Sound Object
OBJ: 11-5
STO: MOUS PP2002 6-2

Lesson 12: Creating a Chart

True/False

1. You can use Undo as many times as needed when working with charts in Microsoft Graph.
ANS: F
OBJ: 12-1
STO: MOUS PP2002 3-1

2. To hide a datasheet, click the View Datasheet button on the Standard toolbar.
ANS: T
OBJ: 12-1
STO: MOUS PP2002 3-1

3. When you switch row and column data, column charts automatically become bar charts.
ANS: F
OBJ: 12-2
STO: MOUS PP2002 3-1

4. You can change the shape of the legend to any AutoShape you want.
ANS: F
OBJ: 12-3
STO: MOUS PP2002 3-1

5. You can use special effects such as textures and gradient fills the same way you use them for other PowerPoint objects.
ANS: T
OBJ: 12-3
STO: MOUS PP2002 3-1

6. In a column chart, the category axis appears on the left side of the chart.
ANS: F
OBJ: 12-5
STO: MOUS PP2002 3-1

7. A legend can be placed anywhere except on the left side of a chart.
ANS: F
OBJ: 12-3
STO: MOUS PP2002 3-1

8. You can change the shape of columns or bars to any AutoShape you choose.
ANS: F
OBJ: 12-4
STO: MOUS PP2002 3-1

9. You can resize pie charts only when they are in 2-D format.
ANS: F
OBJ: 12-6
STO: MOUS PP2002 3-1

10. You can insert text boxes anywhere you want on a chart, except on the left side.
ANS: F
OBJ: 12-4
STO: MOUS PP2002 3-1

11. Axis titles can be formatted as horizontal, vertical, or at a 30-degree angle.
ANS: T
OBJ: 12-3
STO: MOUS PP2002 3-1

12. Numbers on the value axis can be formatted with as many decimal places as you want.
ANS: T
OBJ: 12-3
STO: MOUS PP2002 3-1

13. You can edit chart labels by clicking them with an I-beam pointer.
ANS: T
OBJ: 12-3
STO: MOUS PP2002 3-1

14. When Microsoft Graph is closed, double-click a chart on a slide to edit the chart.
ANS: T
OBJ: 12-2
STO: MOUS PP2002 3-1

15. When you are working with two different types of data, you can combine a pie chart and a line chart into one graph.
ANS: F
OBJ: 12-5
STO: MOUS PP2002 3-1

16. When you create an Excel chart that you want to insert into a PowerPoint slide, you must plan the colors carefully because you can't change them in PowerPoint.
ANS: F
OBJ: 12-7
STO: MOUS PP2002 6-1

17. If you import a multi-sheet Excel file into a PowerPoint slide, you can choose which sheet or chart you want to display on the slide.
ANS: T
OBJ: 12-7
STO: MOUS PP2002 6-1

18. The Drawing toolbar can be used in Microsoft Graph.
ANS: T
OBJ: 12-4
STO: MOUS PP2002 3-1

19. You can animate individual parts of a chart, but you can't add sound effects to the animations.
ANS: F
OBJ: 12-8
STO: MOUS PP2002 3-1

20. After creating a chart in Microsoft Graph, you can return to Slide view by clicking the Slide View button.
ANS: F
OBJ: 12-2
STO: MOUS PP2002 3-1

Multiple Choice

1. To select an entire datasheet:
   a. With the data sheet active, press [Ctrl]+[A]
   b. Click the gray box in the upper-left corner of the datasheet
   c. Choose Select All from the Format menu
   d. a or b
   ANS: d
   OBJ: 12-2
   STO: MOUS PP2002 3-1

2. The unnumbered row above row 1 and the unlettered column to the left of column A are used to:
   a. Select the entire database
   b. Deselect the entire database
   c. Key ordinary data
   d. Key chart labels
   ANS: d
   OBJ: 12-2
   STO: MOUS PP2002 3-1

3. Right-clicking a column head such as A or B:
   a. Selects the column and opens a shortcut menu
   b. Selects the column only
   c. Opens a shortcut menu only
   d. None of the above
   ANS: a
   OBJ: 12-2
   STO: MOUS PP2002 3-1

4. The default chart type is:
   a. Bar
   b. Area
   c. 3-D column
   d. Pie
   ANS: c
   OBJ: 12-1
   STO: MOUS PP2002 3-1

5. The Chart Options dialog box enables you to:
   a. Switch from a column chart format to a bar chart format
   b. Change the scale of a value axis
   c. Insert a chart title
   d. Change the color of the legend
   ANS: c
   OBJ: 12-3
   STO: MOUS PP2002 3-1

6. On a column chart, value axis labels appear on the:
   a. Right side of the chart
   b. Left side of the chart
   c. Top of the chart
   d. Bottom of the chart
   ANS: b
   OBJ: 12-3
   STO: MOUS PP2002 3-1

7. To open the Chart Options dialog box:
   a. Press [Ctrl]+[C]
   b. Choose Chart Options from the Format menu
   c. Point to the edge of the chart, and when you see the Chart Area ScreenTip, right-click the chart area and choose Chart Options
   d. None of the above
   ANS: c
   OBJ: 12-3
   STO: MOUS PP2002 3-1

8. A pie chart:
   a. Is the default chart type
   b. Plots only the first row of data by default
   c. Plots only the last row of data by default
   d. None of the above
   ANS: b
   OBJ: 12-6
   STO: MOUS PP2002 3-1

9. To view a datasheet when Microsoft Graph is active, you can:
   a. Press [Ctrl]+[V]
   b. Click the View Datasheet button
   c. Choose Datasheet from the Format menu
   d. Any of the above
   ANS: b
   OBJ: 12-1
   STO: MOUS PP2002 3-1

10. To change a chart type, you can:
    a. Choose Chart Type from the Chart menu
    b. Choose Chart Type from the Format menu
    c. Press [Ctrl]+[T]
    d. None of the above
    ANS: a
    OBJ: 12-5
    STO: MOUS PP2002 3-1

11. To insert or remove a legend, you can:
    a. Choose Legend from the Format menu
    b. Choose Legend from the Edit menu
    c. Click the Legend tab in the Chart Options dialog box
    d. None of the above
    ANS: c
    OBJ: 12-3
    STO: MOUS PP2002 3-1

12. The currency format:
    a. Displays a dollar sign
    b. Displays commas separating thousands
    c. Can display decimal points
    d. All of the above
    ANS: d
    OBJ: 12-3
    STO: MOUS PP2002 3-1

13. To return to Slide view and close Microsoft Graph:
    a. Press [Shift]+[S]
    b. Click in the slide or gray desktop area outside the chart's border
    c. Choose Slide View from the File menu
    d. None of the above
    ANS: b
    OBJ: 12-1
    STO: MOUS PP2002 3-1

14. To increase the column width in a datasheet, use the:
    a. Two-pointed cross pointer
    b. Four-pointed cross pointer
    c. Cross pointer
    d. Down-arrow pointer
    ANS: a
    OBJ: 12-2
    STO: MOUS PP2002 3-1
15. To add a second value axis to a chart:
    a. You must be working with a 3-D column, bar, or line chart
    b. You cannot be working with a combined chart
    c. You cannot be working on a pie chart
    d. You must be working with more than three data series
    ANS: c
    OBJ: 12-5
    STO: MOUS PP2002 3-1
16. To import a previously created Excel chart onto a PowerPoint slide:
    a. You must use one of the slide layouts that contains a content placeholder or a chart placeholder
    b. Choose Object from the Insert menu and then choose Create from File
    c. Choose Import Excel Chart from the File menu and then choose Create from File
    d. None of the above
    ANS: b
    OBJ: 12-7
    STO: MOUS PP2002 6-1
17. When you double-click an imported Excel chart:
    a. The toolbars and menus change to Excel toolbars and menus
    b. You can change chart numbers, titles, and formatting
    c. You can edit the spreadsheet or chart just as if you were working directly in Excel
    d. All of the above
    ANS: d
    OBJ: 12-7
    STO: MOUS PP2002 6-1
18. To explode a pie slice means to:
    a. Apply an animation effect to just one slice
    b. Change the slice to 3-D
    c. Break up the slide into many smaller slices showing finer detail of the data
    d. Drag the slice out and away from the other slices
    ANS: d
    OBJ: 12-6
    STO: MOUS PP2002 3-1
19. To change the font for all the data labels on a pie chart, first select the labels and then:
    a. Choose Selected Data Labels from the Format menu
    b. Choose Font from the Format menu
    c. Choose a Font from the Font drop-down list on the Formatting toolbar
    d. All of the above
    ANS: d
    OBJ: 12-5
    STO: MOUS PP2002 3-1
20. To select an individual label on a pie chart:
    a. Right-click the desired label and then choose Select from the shortcut menu
    b. Choose the desired label from the Chart Objects drop-down list
    c. First select all the data labels and then click the desired data label
    d. Any of the above
    ANS: c
    OBJ: 12-6
    STO: MOUS PP2002 3-1

Completion

1. A group of data that relates to a common object or category such as product, geographic area, or year is called a _______________.
   ANS: Data series
   OBJ: 12-2
   STO: MOUS PP2002 3-1
2. To open Microsoft Graph within PowerPoint, _____ _____________ the chart icon in the content placeholder.
   ANS: Click
   OBJ: 12-1
   STO: MOUS PP2002 3-1
3. The mouse pointer in a chart datasheet is in the shape of a _______________.
   ANS: White cross
   OBJ: 12-2
   STO: MOUS PP2002 3-1
4. Chart-related buttons are on the Microsoft Graph _______________ toolbar.
   ANS: Standard
   OBJ: 12-1
   STO: MOUS PP2002 3-1
5. Microsoft Graph interprets each row of data as either a data series or a _______________.
   ANS: Category
   OBJ: 12-2
   STO: MOUS PP2002 3-1
6. A _______________ is the box that shows the colors and patterns assigned to each line or column in a chart.
   ANS: Legend
   OBJ: 12-3
   STO: MOUS PP2002 3-1
7. A _______________chart depicts each value as a "slice."
   ANS: Pie
   OBJ: 12-6
   STO: MOUS PP2002 3-1
8. To emphasize a "slice" value, you can drag it away from the other slices. This is called _____________ _____ the slice.
   ANS: Exploding
   OBJ: 12-6
   STO: MOUS PP2002 3-1
9. In formatting the value axis, the _____________ ____ determines the numeric interval between the numbers displayed.
   ANS: Scale
   OBJ: 12-3
   STO: MOUS PP2002 3-1
10. _______________ are small measurement marks, similar to those found on a ruler, that can cross the value axis and category axis.
    ANS: Tick marks
    OBJ: 12-3
    STO: MOUS PP2002 3-1
11. Choose the _______________ option from the Fill Color submenu to apply gradient fills, patterns, or textures to a selected chart object.
    ANS: Fill Effects
    OBJ: 12-3
    STO: MOUS PP2002 3-1

Question Bank

12. You can add a chart to a slide by clicking the ______ ____________ button on the Standard toolbar.
ANS: Insert Chart
OBJ: 12-1
STO: MOUS PP2002 3-1

13. When you place the pointer over different parts of a chart, __________________ appear, identifying the name of each part of the chart.
ANS: ScreenTips
OBJ: 12-3
STO: MOUS PP2002 3-1

14. To select a chart object from a list, click the _______ ___________ list box arrow on the Standard toolbar.
ANS: Chart Objects
OBJ: 12-3
STO: MOUS PP2002 3-1

15. When you want to insert an Excel chart from a file, but you can't remember the exact location or name of the file, click the __________________ button on the Insert Object dialog box.
ANS: Browse
OBJ: 12-7
STO: MOUS PP2002 6-1

16. If you want to change the colors of an imported Excel chart to the presentation's scheme colors, click the __________________ button on the Picture tab of the Format Object dialog box.
ANS: Recolor
OBJ: 12-7
STO: MOUS PP2002 6-1

17. To edit a chart created with Microsoft Graph, ______ ____________.
ANS: Double-click it
OBJ: 12-2
STO: MOUS PP2002 3-1

18. To open a chart imported from Excel to make changes, __________________.
ANS: Double-click it
OBJ: 12-7
STO: MOUS PP2002 6-1

18. To quickly change a chart to a different type, click the __________________ list box arrow on the Microsoft Graph Standard toolbar.
ANS: Chart Type
OBJ: 12-5
STO: MOUS PP2002 3-1

20. If you double-click a legend when Microsoft Graph is active, the __________________ dialog box will open.
ANS: Format Legend
OBJ: 12-3
STO: MOUS PP2002 3-1

Lesson 13: Modifying a PowerPoint Table

True/False

1. You can create a PowerPoint table by choosing Table from the Insert menu.
ANS: T
OBJ: 13-1
STO: MOUS PP2002 3-4

2. The small black down-pointing arrow is used to select a table column.
ANS: T
OBJ: 13-2
STO: MOUS PP2002 3-4

3. The Tables and Borders button is located on the Drawing toolbar.
ANS: F
OBJ: 13-3
STO: MOUS PP2002 3-4

4. When working with a PowerPoint table, you can turn off the pencil pointer by pressing [Esc].
ANS: T
OBJ: 13-1
STO: MOUS PP2002 3-4

5. The only way to make two columns the same width is to measure them by using the ruler.
ANS: F
OBJ: 13-5
STO: MOUS PP2002 3-4

6. When you move the insertion point over the buttons in the Tables and Borders toolbar, ScreenTips appear.
ANS: T
OBJ: 13-1
STO: MOUS PP2002 3-4

7. You can change the height of a table row by dragging the row's top border.
ANS: F
OBJ: 13-5
STO: MOUS PP2002 3-4

8. You cannot format cells in a table by using the shortcut menu.
ANS: F
OBJ: 13-3
STO: MOUS PP2002 3-4

9. When you insert a table column, it is always inserted above the current column.
ANS: F
OBJ: 13-6
STO: MOUS PP2002 3-4

10. In order to change the width of a column, at least one cell in that column must be selected.
ANS: F
OBJ: 13-5
STO: MOUS PP2002 3-4

11. If you want to use Word commands to edit a table created in Word, you must embed the table on a PowerPoint slide.
ANS: T
OBJ: 13-8
STO: MOUS PP2002 6-3

12. You must insert rows or columns one at a time.
ANS: F
OBJ: 13-6
STO: MOUS PP2002 3-4

13. When changing the row height, you can select several rows and drag one row's bottom border to change the row height for all rows.
ANS: F
OBJ: 13-5
STO: MOUS PP2002 3-4

14. To make a group of columns the same width, use the Distribute Columns Evenly button.
ANS: T
OBJ: 13-5
STO: MOUS PP2002 3-4

15. You can insert a Word table by using the Copy and Paste commands.
ANS: T
OBJ: 13-8
STO: MOUS PP2002 6-3

16. To place a right-aligned column of numbers in the center of a column, adjust the right internal margin settings for the cells in the column.
ANS: T
OBJ: 13-4
STO: MOUS PP2002 3-4

17. To change internal margin settings, choose Borders and Fill from the Table menu.
ANS: T
OBJ: 13-4
STO: MOUS PP2002 3-4

18. To eliminate a diagonal border, click it with the Pencil tool.
ANS: F
OBJ: 13-7
STO: MOUS PP2002 3-4

19. You must activate Word to change colors in an imported Word table.
ANS: F
OBJ: 13-8
STO: MOUS PP2002 6-3

20. You must activate Word to change the border style of a group of cells in an imported Word table.
ANS: T
OBJ: 13-8
STO: MOUS PP2002 6-3

Multiple Choice

1. To create a PowerPoint table, you can:
a. Choose Table from the Insert menu
b. Choose Columns and Rows from the Insert menu
c. Click the Insert Table button on the Drawing toolbar
d. All of the above
ANS: a
OBJ: 13-1
STO: MOUS PP2002 3-4

2. To increase the size of all rows and columns proportionately at the same time:
a. Double-click the table's border with the four-pointed arrow
b. Drag one of the table's corner sizing handles
c. Select the entire table, and then drag one of its column borders and one of its row borders
d. None of the above
ANS: b
OBJ: 13-5
STO: MOUS PP2002 3-4

3. To make the middle three rows of a five-row table the same height, select the three rows and then:
a. Drag one of the selected row borders
b. Right-click them
c. Click the Distribute Rows Evenly button
d. All of the above
ANS: c
OBJ: 13-5
STO: MOUS PP2002 3-4

4. You can select an entire column by:
a. Double-clicking the first cell in the column
b. Selecting a cell and then choosing Select Column from the Table menu on the Tables and Borders toolbar
c. Dragging down all the cells in the column
d. b and c
ANS: d
OBJ: 13-2
STO: MOUS PP2002 3-4

5. You can use the Tables and Borders toolbar to:
a. Align text diagonally in a cell
b. Automatically resize columns to fit the text
c. Add fill color to cells
d. b and c
ANS: c
OBJ: 13-2
STO: MOUS PP2002 3-4

6. To vertically center a cell's contents, you can:
a. Press [Ctrl]+[S]
b. Choose Format, then Paragraph, and change the Before spacing value on the Indents and Spacing tab
c. Click the Center Vertically button on the Tables and Borders toolbar
d. All of the above
ANS: c
OBJ: 13-4
STO: MOUS PP2002 3-4

7. To increase the width of a column, you can:
a. Drag a column border
b. Right-click a column border
c. Key the width you want in the Column dialog box
d. All of the above
ANS: a
OBJ: 13-5
STO: MOUS PP2002 3-4

8. Color can be applied to:
a. Borders
b. Cells
c. Text
d. All of the above
ANS: d
OBJ: 13-3
STO: MOUS PP2002 3-4

9. You can use the Pencil tool to:
a. Merge two cells
b. Increase the height of a row
c. Remove or change the border between two cells
d. All of the above
ANS: c
OBJ: 13-7
STO: MOUS PP2002 3-4

10. You can use the Eraser tool to:
a. Merge two cells
b. Remove text from a cell
c. Remove the color from a cell's border
d. a and b
ANS: a
OBJ: 13-7
STO: MOUS PP2002 3-4

11. In a table, fill refers to:
a. Color for text
b. Color or texture for a cell
c. Line style
d. None of the above
ANS: b
OBJ: 13-3
STO: MOUS PP2002 3-4

12. When you split a cell diagonally:
a. The result is one cell with a diagonal line drawn through it
b. You need to use text boxes to insert text in the triangular cells that result
c. You create two triangular cells that can be independently formatted
d. a and b
ANS: a
OBJ: 13-7
STO: MOUS PP2002 3-4

13. To select an active table by using the keyboard:
    a. Press [Shift]+[S]
    b. Press [Ctrl]+[A]
    c. Press [Alt]+[5] on the numeric keyboard
    d. None of the above
    ANS: b
    OBJ: 13-2
    STO: MOUS PP2002 3-4
14. You can embed a Word table on a PowerPoint slide by:
    a. Copying the Word table to the clipboard and then pasting it on a PowerPoint slide
    b. Choosing Word Table from PowerPoint's Insert Table dialog box
    c. Choosing Picture from the Insert menu
    d. a or c
    ANS: a
    OBJ: 13-8
    STO: MOUS PP2002 6-3
15. If you use the Paste Special command when copying a Word table onto a PowerPoint slide, you can:
    a. Recolor table elements by using the PowerPoint Recolor command
    b. Double-click the table to make changes to it in Word
    c. Apply fill effects to individual cells when Word is active
    d. All of the above
    ANS: d
    OBJ: 13-8
    STO: MOUS PP2002 6-3
16. If you want to be able to activate Word to edit a Word table that you copy and paste into PowerPoint, you must:
    a. Use the Paste Special command when you copy it
    b. Press [Ctrl]+[V] to copy it
    c. Drag the table from Word to PowerPoint
    d. a or c
    ANS: a
    OBJ: 13-8
    STO: MOUS PP2002 6-3
17. To center a row of text or numbers vertically within the row, select all the cells and then:
    a. Click the Center Align button on the Formatting toolbar
    b. Increase the number of points in the Before Paragraph setting in the Format Paragraph dialog box
    c. Click the Center Vertically button on the Tables and Borders toolbar
    d. Right-click the selection and choose Borders and Fill from the shortcut menu
    ANS: c
    OBJ: 13-4
    STO: MOUS PP2002 3-4
18. If you left-align a column of words, but they appear in the center of the cells rather than at the left edge, the problem is most likely that:
    a. The cells were previously formatted as Center Only
    b. You are working on a read-only table
    c. The left internal margin is set too wide
    d. None of the above; try again
    ANS: c
    OBJ: 13-4
    STO: MOUS PP2002 3-4
19. If you want the text in the first cell of the first row centered across the entire width of the table:
    a. Select the row, merge the cells, and then click the Center button on the Tables and Borders toolbar
    b. Select the row, merge the cells, and then click the Center button on the Formatting toolbar
    c. Select the row, choose No Borders from the Borders submenu, and then click the Center button on the Formatting toolbar
    d. Delete the row, make a single-cell table the same width as the table, place it directly above the table, and then key the text and click the Center button on the Formatting toolbar
    ANS: a
    OBJ: 13-7
    STO: MOUS PP2002 3-4
20. To delete an entire row:
    a. Select all the cells in the row and press [Delete]
    b. Place the insertion point in any word in the row, and then choose Delete Rows from the Table menu on the Tables and Borders toolbar
    c. Right-click any text in the row and then choose Delete Rows from the shortcut menu
    d. b or c
    ANS: d
    OBJ: 13-6
    STO: MOUS PP2002 3-4

Completion

1. To combine two or more cells into one cell, you ________________ the cells.
   ANS: Merge
   OBJ: 13-7
   STO: MOUS PP2002 3-4
2. Use the ________________ button to divide a table cell into two smaller cells.
   ANS: Split Cell
   OBJ: 13-7
   STO: MOUS PP2002 3-4
3. When you specify the amount of space between a cell's border and its text, you are changing one or more of the cell's ________________.
   ANS: Margins
   OBJ: 13-4
   STO: MOUS PP2002 3-4
4. In a table, the blinking insertion point indicates the ________________ cell.
   ANS: Active or Selected
   OBJ: 13-2
   STO: MOUS PP2002 3-4
5. To move to the next cell in a table by using your keyboard, press ________________.
   ANS: [Tab] or [Right Arrow]
   OBJ: 13-2
   STO: MOUS PP2002 3-4
6. You can select an entire table by choosing Select Table from the Table menu on the ________________ toolbar.
   ANS: Tables and Borders
   OBJ: 13-2
   STO: MOUS PP2002 3-4
7. To make all columns in a table the same width, you can use the ________________ button.
   ANS: Distribute Columns Evenly
   OBJ: 13-5
   STO: MOUS PP2002 3-4
8. You can change a cell's font color by selecting the cell and clicking the ________________ button on the Drawing toolbar.
   ANS: Font Color
   OBJ: 13-3
   STO: MOUS PP2002 3-4

9. You can change a cell's fill color by clicking the Fill Color button on the Drawing toolbar or the ________ ________________ toolbar.
ANS: Tables and Borders
OBJ: 13-3
STO: MOUS PP2002 3-4

10. You can select an entire table by clicking its _______ ____________.
ANS: Border
OBJ: 13-2
STO: MOUS PP2002 3-4

11. To split a cell diagonally use the ________________ tool.
ANS: Pencil
OBJ: 13-7
STO: MOUS PP2002 3-4

12. If a cell is not wide enough for the text you are keying in it, the text will ________________________.
ANS: Wrap to a new line
OBJ: 13-1
STO: MOUS PP2002 3-4

13. If a cell is not wide enough for the text you are keying in it, the row containing the cell will become __________________.
ANS: Higher or Taller
OBJ: 13-1
STO: MOUS PP2002 3-4

14. If you want to remove a single cell in a table, you must __________________ with another cell.
ANS: Merge it
OBJ: 13-7
STO: MOUS PP2002 3-4

15. To remove a table imported from Word, select the table and then press __________________.
ANS: [Delete]
OBJ: 13-8
STO: MOUS PP2002 6-3

16. If you are using a table to make a calendar, and you want to have two dates share a cell, you can use the __________________ to draw a diagonal border in the cell.
ANS: Pencil or Pencil tool
OBJ: 13-7
STO: MOUS PP2002 3-4

17. If you want to change the border style for some cells in a table, choose the border style, thickness, and color from the Tables and Borders toolbar, and then click each border that you want to change with the __________________.
ANS: Pencil tool
OBJ: 13-4
STO: MOUS PP2002 3-4

18. When you finish keying text in the last column of the last row of a table, press __________________ on your keyboard to insert a new row.
ANS: [Tab]
OBJ: 13-6
STO: MOUS PP2002 3-4

19. You can click the Table button on the ____________ _______ toolbar as another way to create a table.
ANS: Standard
OBJ: 13-1
STO: MOUS PP2002 3-4

20. To make several columns the same width, first select the columns and then click the __________________ ______ button.
ANS: Distribute Evenly
OBJ: 13-5
STO: MOUS PP2002 3-4

Lesson 14: Flowcharts, Organization Charts, and Diagrams

True/False

1. PowerPoint provides special AutoShapes that are designed for flowcharts.
ANS: T
OBJ: 14-1
STO: MOUS PP2002 3-1

2. You can use connector lines only with Flowchart AutoShapes.
ANS: F
OBJ: 14-1
STO: MOUS PP2002 3-1

3. Column Chart is one of the options available in the Diagram Gallery dialog box.
ANS: F
OBJ: 14-6
STO: MOUS PP2002 3-1

4. When you rearrange AutoShapes on a slide, the connector lines stay attached and adjust to the new position of the AutoShapes they connect to.
ANS: T
OBJ: 14-1
STO: MOUS PP2002 3-1

5. A Radial diagram is used to show a process with a continuous cycle
ANS: F
OBJ: 14-6
STO: MOUS PP2002 3-1

6. Flowchart shapes can be drawn, positioned, and formatted just like any other AutoShapes.
ANS: T
OBJ: 14-1
STO: MOUS PP2002 3-1

7. One way to create a Radial diagram is to start with one of the Content slide layouts.
ANS: T
OBJ: 14-6
STO: MOUS PP2002 3-1

8. You can stack boxes vertically in an org chart if you need more horizontal space.
ANS: T
OBJ: 14-4
STO: MOUS PP2002 3-1

9. A selection rectangle enables you to select several org chart boxes on different levels all at one time.
ANS: T
OBJ: 14-3
STO: MOUS PP2002 3-1

10. You can demote or promote boxes in an org chart.
ANS: T
OBJ: 14-4
STO: MOUS PP2002 3-1

11. The Assistant button on the Org Chart toolbar is used to add subordinate workers under a manager.
ANS: F
OBJ: 14-3
STO: MOUS PP2002 3-1

12. You open the Align or Distribute submenu from the Draw menu.
ANS: T
OBJ: 14-1
STO: MOUS PP2002 3-1

13. Flowchart connectors can point at odd angles or can be aligned horizontally or vertically.

ANS: T
OBJ: 14-1
STO: MOUS PP2002 3-1

14. In an org chart, a coworker box is one that is inserted on the same level as the currently selected box.
ANS: T
OBJ: 14-4
STO: MOUS PP2002 3-1

15. You cannot mix curved and straight connector lines on a flowchart.
ANS: F
OBJ: 14-1
STO: MOUS PP2002 3-1

16. A Radial diagram is most often used to illustrate overlapping relationships.
ANS: F
OBJ: 14-6
STO: MOUS PP2002 3-1

17. You can key as many lines of text as you like in an org chart box.
ANS: T
OBJ: 14-2
STO: MOUS PP2002 3-1

18. You can key an unlimited amount of text in a flow-chart AutoShape.
ANS: T
OBJ: 14-1
STO: MOUS PP2002 3-1

19. Org chart boxes have a much narrower range of fill effect options and fill colors than flowchart shapes.
ANS: F
OBJ: 14-5
STO: MOUS PP2002 3-1

20. When working with an org chart or diagram, turning off AutoLayout changes the diagram's elements to AutoShapes and connector lines.
ANS: T
OBJ: 14-1
STO: MOUS PP2002 3-1

Multiple Choice

1. In flowcharts, the following shape is traditionally used to signify a decision-making point, where "Yes" and "No" take different paths:
a. Square
b. Diamond
c. Rectangle
d. Circle
ANS: b
OBJ: 14-1
STO: MOUS PP2002 3-1

2. When you start a new org chart, you begin with a default chart template with the following number of boxes:
a. 1
b. 2
c. 4
d. 10
ANS: c
OBJ: 14-2
STO: MOUS PP2002 3-1

3. The shape of an org chart box is:
a. A rounded rectangle
b. A square
c. Whatever shape you choose
d. A circle
ANS: c
OBJ: 14-5
STO: MOUS PP2002 3-1

4. In an org chart, if Mary, Tom, and Joe all report to the same person, their relationship to each other is:
a. Coworker
b. Assistant
c. Subordinate
d. Superior
ANS: a
OBJ: 14-3
STO: MOUS PP2002 3-1

5. To promote an org chart box:
a. Drag it on top of a box that already exists at the desired level
b. Right-click the box and choose Promote
c. Drag it on top of the box that will be its new superior
d. Insert a new box on the desired level and then drag the box to be promoted on top of the new box
ANS: c
OBJ: 14-4
STO: MOUS PP2002 3-1

6. To freely move individual org chart boxes, you must first:
a. Ungroup the org chart
b. Create an org chart look-alike by using AutoShapes and connector lines
c. Turn off AutoLayout
d. None of the above
ANS: c
OBJ: 14-5
STO: MOUS PP2002 3-1

7. To move between boxes in an org chart, press:
a. [Enter]
b. The arrow keys
c. [Ctrl]+arrow keys
d. [Tab]
ANS: b
OBJ: 14-3
STO: MOUS PP2002 3-1

8. An org chart branch is:
a. All the subordinate boxes that report up to a single superior
b. Another name for an org chart level
c. The place where you put extra positions that don't fit anywhere else
d. A break in the chart so it can continue on a new slide
ANS: a
OBJ: 14-4
STO: MOUS PP2002 3-1

9. In a Radial diagram:
a. You are limited to 12 or fewer circles
b. You can change from circles to another AutoShape, but all shapes must be the same
c. You can change the color of the shapes but not the connector lines
d. None of the above
ANS: d
OBJ: 14-6
STO: MOUS PP2002 3-1

10. To delete a selected org chart box by using the keyboard, press:
a. [Ctrl]+[X]
b. [Delete]
c. [Shift]+[X]
d. [Shift]+[V]
ANS: b
OBJ: 14-3
STO: MOUS PP2002 3-1

11. To select multiple boxes in an org chart that are not next to one another, click each of the desired boxes while pressing:
    a. [Ctrl]+[Alt]
    b. [Shift]
    c. [Alt]
    d. a or b
    ANS: b
    OBJ: 14-3
    STO: MOUS PP2002 3-1
12. A red endpoint on a connector line indicates a(n):
    a. Locked connector
    b. Unlocked connector
    c. AutoShape with no connection sites
    d. Invalid connector
    ANS: b
    OBJ: 14-1
    STO: MOUS PP2002 3-1
13. You can change the following attributes in an org chart box:
    a. Border color
    b. Box color
    c. Text color
    d. All of the above
    ANS: d
    OBJ: 14-5
    STO: MOUS PP2002 3-1
14. When AutoLayout is turned on, selected org chart or diagram shapes are indicated by:
    a. Blinking borders
    b. White sizing handles
    c. Yellow diamond adjustment handles
    d. Gray sizing handles
    ANS: d
    OBJ: 14-5
    STO: MOUS PP2002 3-1
15. You can change the look of a group of org chart boxes by:
    a. Applying a shadow to the boxes and changing the shadow color
    b. Applying a double-line border to the boxes and changing the border color
    c. Applying a gradient fill to the boxes
    d. All of the above
    ANS: d
    OBJ: 14-6
    STO: MOUS PP2002 3-1
16. If you want to use the keyboard to navigate from the third level of one org chart branch to the third level of the branch to the right:
    a. Use [Alt]+[Right Arrow] to jump to the next branch
    b. Use [Ctrl]+[Right Arrow] to jump to the next branch
    c. You must use the [Up Arrow] to travel up one branch and then the [Down Arrow] to travel down the other branch
    d. You must use your mouse to move to the other branch
    ANS: c
    OBJ: 14-2
    STO: MOUS PP2002 3-1
17. You can draw several connector lines without re-clicking the connector button each time you start a new line by:
    a. Holding down [Ctrl] while you draw a connector
    b. Double-clicking the connector button
    c. Double-clicking a connector after it is drawn
    d. Holding down [Alt] while you draw a connector
    ANS: b
    OBJ: 14-2
    STO: MOUS PP2002 3-1
18. Connection sites appear on a flowchart shape when you:
    a. Select the shape
    b. Point to the shape with the arrow pointer
    c. Hold down [Shift] while you draw a connector
    d. Double-click the shape
    ANS: b
    OBJ: 14-1
    STO: MOUS PP2002 3-1
19. If one or more yellow diamonds appear on a connector line when you select it:
    a. You need to reconnect the end points to the shapes on either side of it
    b. You can drag the yellow diamonds to change the shape of the connector line
    c. You can insert a new shape between the yellow diamonds
    d. You can double-click a yellow diamond to break the connection to the nearest shape
    ANS: b
    OBJ: 14-1
    STO: MOUS PP2002 3-1
20. When a blinking insertion point is present in an org chart or diagram box, you can move to the previous box by pressing the following key(s):
    a. [Esc], [Shift]+[Tab]
    b. [Shift]+[Tab]
    c. [Alt]+[Shift]+[Tab]
    d. You must use your mouse to move to a different box
    ANS: a
    OBJ: 14-2
    STO: MOUS PP2002 3-1

Completion

1. A(n) __________________ is a diagram used to show a sequence of events, such as instructions for planting a tree.
   ANS: Flowchart
   OBJ: 14-1
   STO: MOUS PP2002 3-1
2. A(n) ________________________ is a diagram typically used in business to show who reports to whom and who is responsible for what function or task.
   ANS: Organizational chart or Org chart
   OBJ: 14-2
   STO: MOUS PP2002 3-1
3. __________________ are used to link the shapes in a flowchart.
   ANS: Connector lines
   OBJ: 14-2
   STO: MOUS PP2002 3-1
4. When you are working with AutoShapes and connector lines, the small blue handles that appear on AutoShapes are called __________________.
   ANS: Connection sites
   OBJ: 14-1
   STO: MOUS PP2002 3-1
5. You can change an AutoShape by choosing Change AutoShape from the __________________ menu.
   ANS: Draw
   OBJ: 14-1
   STO: MOUS PP2002 3-1
6. A __________________ diagram is used to show foundation-based relationships.
   ANS: Pyramid

OBJ: 14-6
STO: MOUS PP2002 3-1

7. Each chart box in an org chart is positioned on a ________________ in the chart that indicates its position in the hierarchy of the organization.
ANS: Level or Line
OBJ: 14-4
STO: MOUS PP2002 3-1

8. The top box in an org chart is level ____________.
ANS: 1
OBJ: 14-3
STO: MOUS PP2002 3-1

9. Use the ____________________ commands to align and evenly space flowchart shapes.
ANS: Align and Distribute
OBJ: 14-1
STO: MOUS PP2002 3-1

10. An org chart box placed between a superior box and subordinate boxes is called a(n) ______________ box.
ANS: Assistant
OBJ: 14-3
STO: MOUS PP2002 3-1

11. An org chart box that has subordinates connected to it is called a(n) ________________ box.
ANS: Superior
OBJ: 14-3
STO: MOUS PP2002 3-1

12. To add an assistant to a selected org chart box, click the list box arrow for the ________________ button on the Organization Chart toolbar.
ANS: Insert Shape
OBJ: 14-3
STO: MOUS PP2002 3-1

13. The ________________ arrow connector automatically bends as needed to make a path between two shapes.
ANS: Elbow or Curved
OBJ: 14-1
STO: MOUS PP2002 3-1

14. When keying text in an org chart or diagram box, press ________________ to start a new line within the box.
ANS: [Enter] or [Shift]+[Enter]
OBJ: 14-2
STO: MOUS PP2002 3-1

15. You can draw a flowchart shape by choosing Flowchart from the ________________menu.
ANS: AutoShapes
OBJ: 14-1
STO: MOUS PP2002 3-1

16. To help you arrange flowchart shapes and connectors, use the ________________ floating toolbar from the Draw menu.
ANS: Align or Distribute
OBJ: 14-2
STO: MOUS PP2002 3-1

17. Flowcharts are diagrams used to show __________ ____________________ in a process.
ANS: A sequence of events (steps)
OBJ: 14-1
STO: MOUS PP2002 3-1

18. Organizational charts are used mainly to show the ________________ arrangement of people in an organization.
ANS: Hierarchical
OBJ: 14-2
STO: MOUS PP2002 3-1

19. If your org chart has too many boxes to fit across a page, you can arrange them ________________.
ANS: Vertically
OBJ: 14-4
STO: MOUS PP2002 3-1

20. A secretary to the president or head of a business is usually shown in a(n) ________________ box.
ANS: Assistant
OBJ: 14-3
STO: MOUS PP2002 3-1

Lesson 15: Distributing and Presenting Your Work

True/False

1. Meeting Minder can be used to remind you when you are scheduled to make a presentation.
ANS: F
OBJ: 15-1
STO: MOUS PP2002 7-2

2. Presentations that use timings to automatically advance to the next slide are usually not appropriate for live presentations.
ANS: T
OBJ: 15-1
STO: MOUS PP2002 7-2

3. You can open the Meeting Minder dialog box during a presentation from the shortcut menu.
ANS: T
OBJ: 15-1
STO: MOUS PP2002 7-2

4. You can print meeting minutes by using the PowerPoint Print dialog box.
ANS: F
OBJ: 15-1
STO: MOUS PP2002 7-2

5. When you export meeting minutes to Word, they are saved in Rich Text Format.
ANS: T
OBJ: 15-1
STO: MOUS PP2002 7-2

6. PowerPoint presentations can be converted into color overhead transparencies, but not into 35mm color slides.
ANS: F
OBJ: 15-3
STO: MOUS PP2002 7-2

7. You cannot display animations if you are using overhead transparencies.
ANS: T
OBJ: 15-2
STO: MOUS PP2002 7-2

8. When you send a presentation for a review, reviewers can make changes and comments without affecting the original presentation.
ANS: T
OBJ: 15-4
STO: MOUS PP2002 8-1

9. PowerPoint has all the tools needed to broadcast a presentation live over the Internet.
ANS: F
OBJ: 15-6
STO: MOUS PP2002 8-3

10. If you have a microphone, you can record voice narration for a presentation that you are saving for an online broadcast.
ANS: T
OBJ: 15-6
STO: MOUS PP2002 8-4

11. Pack and Go compresses and manages large presentation files so that they can be stored on one or more floppy disks.
ANS: T
OBJ: 15-2
STO: MOUS PP2002 7-6

12. When you embed the TrueType fonts that your presentation is using, the presentation can use those fonts on a different computer, even if that computer doesn't have the required fonts installed.
ANS: T
OBJ: 15-2
STO: MOUS PP2002 7-4

13. When you unpack a Pack and Go file, the Pack and Go Wizard determines where the unpacked file will be saved.
ANS: F
OBJ: 15-2
STO: MOUS PP2002 7-6

14. To format a presentation for the Web, choose Convert to Web Page from the Tools menu.
ANS: F
OBJ: 15-5
STO: MOUS PP2002 7-5

15. When you format a presentation for the Web, you can choose to include all slides or just specific slides that you select.
ANS: T
OBJ: 15-5
STO: MOUS PP2002 7-5

16. When formatting a presentation for the Web, if you choose to format it for all browsers, it will be a larger file than if you choose to format it for only the latest versions of Internet Explorer.
ANS: T
OBJ: 15-5
STO: MOUS PP2002 7-5

17. When viewing a presentation in a browser, a list of slide titles can be displayed on the left side of the page.
ANS: T
OBJ: 15-5
STO: MOUS PP2002 7-5

18. If you see a hand icon when pointing to text on a Web page, the text is a hyperlink to another page.
ANS: T
OBJ: 15-5
STO: MOUS PP2002 7-5

19. When you merge reviewers' copies of a presentation with the original, the changes the reviewers made are automatically applied to the presentation.
ANS: F
OBJ: 15-4
STO: MOUS PP2002 8-2

20. If you are thinking about using a presentation on the Web, you can preview it as a Web page before saving it in HTML format.
ANS: T
OBJ: 15-5
STO: MOUS PP2002 7-5

Multiple Choice

1. Meeting Minder is used during a presentation to:
a. Record audience comments and other notes in the form of meeting minutes
b. Create a new slide titled "To Do List" while the presentation is progressing
c. Create a new slide titled "Action Items" while the presentation is progressing
d. a and c
ANS: d
OBJ: 15-1
STO: MOUS PP2002 7-2

2. If you use Meeting Minder during a slide show, you can give the audience a copy of the meeting minutes by:
a. Printing or e-mailing the Meeting Minutes slide created automatically during the presentation
b. Exporting the Meeting Minutes to Word and then printing or e-mailing them
c. Printing or e-mailing audience handouts, which will include the Meeting Minutes slide created automatically during the presentation
d. All of the above
ANS: b
OBJ: 15-1
STO: MOUS PP2002 7-2

3. You can open the Meeting Minder dialog box to take notes during a presentation by:
a. Pressing [Alt]+[M]
b. Right-clicking anywhere on the slide and choosing Meeting Minder from the shortcut menu
c. Clicking the special Meeting Minder action button that automatically appears during a slide show set to advance manually
d. All of the above
ANS: b
OBJ: 15-1
STO: MOUS PP2002 7-2

4. Slides sized for an On-screen Show have the same proportions as slides sized for:
a. Banners
b. 35mm slides
c. Overheads
d. b and c
ANS: c
OBJ: 15-3
STO: MOUS PP2002 7-2

5. If you want to save a large presentation to a floppy disk but find that it is too large to fit on one disk, you should:
a. Break your presentation into two or more separate presentations that are small enough to fit
b. Use Pack and Go to compress your presentation
c. E-mail your presentation to a service bureau
d. All of the above
ANS: b
OBJ: 15-2
STO: MOUS PP2002 7-6

6. Animation effects will be lost if you:
a. Deliver your presentation by using 35mm slides
b. Disable automatic slide advances when conducting a live meeting
c. Forget to save your presentation after you create an Action Items slide
d. All of the above
ANS: a
OBJ: 15-3
STO: MOUS PP2002 7-2

7. To insert a reviewer's comment in a presentation:
 a. You must be hooked up with a microphone
 b. You key it in the Notes pane
 c. Click the Insert Comment button on the Reviewing toolbar
 d. b or c
 ANS: c
 OBJ: 15-4
 STO: MOUS PP2002 8-2

8. To save a presentation as a Web page, choose:
 a. Convert to HTML from the Tools menu
 b. Save as HTML from the File menu
 c. Save as Web Page from the File menu
 d. Set Up Show from the Slide Show menu
 ANS: c
 OBJ: 15-5
 STO: MOUS PP2002 7-5

9. When the Save As dialog box is open, you can change the file format to HTML by:
 a. Choosing Web Page from the Save As Type drop-down list
 b. Choosing Hyperlink Page from the Save As Type drop-down list
 c. Closing the Save As dialog box and opening the Convert to HTML dialog box instead
 d. Closing the Save As dialog box and opening the Set Up Show dialog box instead
 ANS: a
 OBJ: 15-5
 STO: MOUS PP2002 7-5

10. When the Publish as Web Page dialog box is open, you can:
 a. Choose which browsers will be supported by the resulting HTML file
 b. Key an actual Web site address in the File Name text box if you have one available to you
 c. Choose which slides will be available in the resulting HTML file
 d. All of the above
 ANS: d
 OBJ: 15-5
 STO: MOUS PP2002 7-5

11. When you record and save a broadcast for later viewing:
 a. You can save it wherever you want
 b. You must have read/write access to a shared folder
 c. You must have a microphone attached to your computer
 d. a and c
 ANS: a
 OBJ: 15-6
 STO: MOUS PP2002 8-3

12. To make speaker notes available on a Web page:
 a. Choose the Display Speaker-Notes option in the Set Up Show dialog box
 b. Choose Speaker Notes in the Save File as Type drop-down menu
 c. Choose the Display Speaker Notes option in the Publish as Web Page dialog box
 d. You can't make speaker notes available on a Web page
 ANS: c
 OBJ: 15-5
 STO: MOUS PP2002 7-5

13. Comments that reviewers add to a presentation:
 a. Are not displayed when viewed as a slide show
 b. Cannot be deleted
 c. Change the presentation if you accept them
 d. All of the above
 ANS: a
 OBJ: 15-4
 STO: MOUS PP2002 8-1

14. To unpack a Pack and Go presentation:
 a. Use Windows Explorer to run the pngsetup.exe application
 b. Open PowerPoint, choose Unpack from the Tools menu, and navigate to the A: drive or other location where the pngsetup.exe file is stored
 c. Click the Windows Start button, choose Run, click the Browse button, and locate the pngsetup.exe file
 d. a or c
 ANS: d
 OBJ: 15-2
 STO: MOUS PP2002 7-6

15. Options that you can choose when running the Pack and Go Wizard are:
 a. Whether to embed TrueType fonts
 b. Where the resulting Pack and Go file will be saved
 c. How many floppy disks to use
 d. a and b
 ANS: d
 OBJ: 15-2
 STO: MOUS PP2002 7-6

16. Transparency film is used:
 a. To make 35mm slides from your presentation
 b. To make an AutoShape or other object transparent when it's placed on top of text
 c. In a printer to print slides that can be used with an overhead projector
 d. In front of the lens of a projection unit to correct presentation color settings
 ANS: c
 OBJ: 15-3
 STO: MOUS PP2002 7-2

17. When you change the Page Setup options for a completed presentation from On-screen Show to 35mm slides:
 a. You must carefully edit each slide to correct the color scheme changes that occur
 b. You must change all the fonts to a smaller size to fit the new slide size
 c. You might need to make some minor adjustments to the proportions of clip art and other graphic images
 d. PowerPoint automatically adjusts the size and proportions of all visual elements in the presentation
 ANS: c
 OBJ: 15-3
 STO: MOUS PP2002 7-2

18. To print the comments that are contained in a presentation:
 a. Choose Comments from the Print What list box in the Print dialog box
 b. Check the Include Comment Pages option in the Print dialog box and then print at least one slide or notes page
 c. Right-click one of the comments and choose Print from the shortcut menu
 d. Choose Notes Pages from the Print What list box in the Print dialog box
 ANS: d
 OBJ: 15-1
 STO: MOUS PP2002 6-2

19. If you want to export meeting minutes when the Export button is dimmed:
    a. Double-click a meeting minutes entry to activate the Export button
    b. Double-click the Export button
    c. Click an action item to activate the Export button
    d. The presentation file is corrupt and the Export option is no longer available

    ANS: c
    OBJ: 15-1
    STO: MOUS PP2002 7-2

20. When you create action items during a presentation:
    a. All the action items are collected on a slide with the title "Summary" at the end of the presentation
    b. You can create a slide listing all the action items by choosing the Action Item slide from the slide show's shortcut menu
    c. An attractive slide is inserted at the end of the presentation listing all the action items that you entered
    d. A slide with the title "Action Items" is inserted at the end of the presentation, but it needs to be formatted to match the presentation

    ANS: c
    OBJ: 15-1
    STO: MOUS PP2002 7-2

Completion

1. A ________________ is software that enables you to view Web pages.
   ANS: Browser
   OBJ: 15-5
   STO: MOUS PP2002 7-5
2. To prepare an existing PowerPoint presentation for publication on the Web, choose the ____________ ________ command from the File menu.
   ANS: Save as Web Page
   OBJ: 15-5
   STO: MOUS PP2002 7-5
3. Slide timings are most appropriate for __________ _______ presentations.
   ANS: Self-running or Kiosk
   OBJ: 15-1
   STO: MOUS PP2002 7-2
4. While presenting a slide show, if you want to assign a task to a participant, click the ______________ tab on the Meeting Minder dialog box.
   ANS: Action Items
   OBJ: 15-1
   STO: MOUS PP2002 7-2
5. When you export meeting minutes to Word, a document is created in ________________________ format.
   ANS: Rich Text Format (.rtf)
   OBJ: 15-1
   STO: MOUS PP2002 7-2
6. To make your own overhead transparencies, insert ____________________ in your printer.
   ANS: Transparency film
   OBJ: 15-2
   STO: MOUS PP2002 5-3
7. The size of slides formatted for an on-screen presentation is ____________________.
   ANS: 7.5 by 10 inches or 10 by 7.5 inches
   OBJ: 15-3
   STO: MOUS PP2002 7-2
8. The orientation of a slide that is taller than it is wide is ________________.
   ANS: Portrait
   OBJ: 15-3
   STO: MOUS PP2002 7-2
9. A 35mm slide format is ________________ (wider/narrower) than an on-screen slide format.
   ANS: Wider
   OBJ: 15-3
   STO: MOUS PP2002 7-2
10. If an audience sees your presentation over the Internet at the same time that you are broadcasting it, they are viewing it in ________________.
    ANS: Real time
    OBJ: 15-6
    STO: MOUS PP2002 8-4
11. The first page that you see when you play a presentation broadcast is called the ________________.
    ANS: Lobby page
    OBJ: 15-6
    STO: MOUS PP2002 8-4
12. The name of the file that you need to run to unpack a Pack and Go presentation is ________________.
    ANS: Pngsetup or Pngsetup.exe
    OBJ: 15-2
    STO: MOUS PP2002 7-6
13. If you are creating a Pack and Go file, and you want to be sure that text is displayed with the correct fonts on someone else's computer, choose the _____ ______________ option.
    ANS: Embed TrueType Fonts
    OBJ: 15-2
    STO: MOUS PP2002 7-6
14. If you need to see how your presentation will appear as a Web page without first saving it as a Web page, choose ____________________ from the File menu.
    ANS: Web Page Preview
    OBJ: 15-5
    STO: MOUS PP2002 7-5
15. To embed fonts within a presentation choose Save Options from the Tools menu in the ____________ _____ dialog box.
    ANS: Save As
    OBJ: 15-2
    STO: MOUS PP2002 7-4
16. If you are viewing a PowerPoint presentation on Internet Explorer 5, click the ________________ ____ button to see a list of slide titles.
    ANS: Show/Hide Outline
    OBJ: 15-5
    STO: MOUS PP2002 7-5
17. An Internet-like system that exists only within a company or organization is called ____________ ____.
    ANS: An intranet
    OBJ: 15-5
    STO: MOUS PP2002 7-5
18. When working in Slide view, you can open the Meeting Minder dialog box from the ______________ menu.
    ANS: Tools
    OBJ: 15-1
    STO: MOUS PP2002 7-2
19. When you click the Export button in the Meeting Minder dialog box, you have the option of sending the information to Microsoft Outlook or to _______ __________.
    ANS: Microsoft Word

Question Bank

OBJ: 15-1
STO: MOUS PP2002 7-2

20. You can use a ________________ to transform your presentation into 35mm slides, full-color printed handouts, and other printed or photographic materials.
ANS: Service bureau
OBJ: 15-3
STO: MOUS PP2002 7-2

Unit Exams

Introduction

The Unit Exams for Margaret Marple's *PowerPoint 2002: Comprehensive* text contain the following assessment materials:

Exams

EXAM	COURSE MATERIAL COVERED
Exam 1	Unit 1 (Lessons 1-2)
Exam 2	Unit 2 (Lessons 3-5)
Exam 3	Unit 3 (Lessons 6-8)
Exam 4	Unit 4 (Lessons 9-11)
Exam 5	Unit 5 (Lessons 12-14)
Exam 6	Unit 6 (Lesson 15)

Each exam is divided into two parts—"Questions" and "Applications." Testing time for each part is 45 minutes. You can administer the test in one 90-minute period or over two 45-minute periods. (In some circumstances it may be necessary to allow slightly more time for your students to complete the various parts of the exams. Use your judgement as to what students can reasonably accomplish given your particular circumstances.)

All of the exams in this booklet can be photocopied for distribution to your students. You can also print a specific exam file (see "Files on the CD" below).

Exam Keys and Solutions

Following the exams are the exam keys, which contain answers to the short-answer questions. After the exam keys are representations of the solution files that students are asked to produce. As with the *Solutions Manual,* your students' solution files may differ from those in this booklet due to differences in printers and pagination.

Make sure students place their names, initials, or other identifiers on any printouts they turn in as part of an exam.

Files on the CD

The "Unit Exams" folder on the enclosed CD contains the following five folders:

- "Exams"– Contains the actual unit exams in a Word format, which you can print for your students. You can also modify the exams to suit the needs of your particular class.
- "Keys"– Contains the answer keys files for the "Questions" portion of the exams.
- "Student Files"– Contains the files which students require to work through the "Applications" portion of the exams.
- "Solutions"– Contains solutions files for the "Applications" portion of the exams.
- "Checklists"– Contains an "Assessment Checklist" for each exam (see next page).

Loading Student Files

You'll need to make the following student files from the CD available to your students at the start of the "Applications" portion of the exam:

EXAM	FILE
Exam 1	None
Exam 2	ResForms
Exam 3	None
Exam 4	JobFair4
Exam 5	None
Exam 6	RetR1, RetOrig

Assessment Checklists

An "Assessment Checklist" for each exam is included in this Section and on the enclosed CD. Each checklist indicates the lessons covered by a specific exam, assigns a point value to each question and procedural step, and provides an assessment guide to help you assign a percentage grade. Assessment Checklists are Word files. You can change the point values for a questions or procedures to meet the needs of your class.

For more information about the Assessment Checklists and assessment strategies, see the Projects Manual.

NAME: ______________________ CLASS: ______________________

Exam 1

Questions

Answer the following questions. You can use your computer during the exam. Remember to monitor the amount of time remaining in the period.

1. Name the two toolbars that appear at the top of the screen by default when you open PowerPoint.

2. Where are the View buttons located on-screen?

3. If a lightbulb icon appears somewhere on a slide, what does it mean?

4. How do you display a ScreenTip?

5. What shape is the mouse pointer when it's inside a text placeholder?

6. What shape is the mouse pointer when it's outside of a text placeholder and not on any other object?

7. When you are viewing a presentation in Normal view, what does the Page Down key do?

8. Which button do you click to send a presentation directly to the printer using previously defined settings?

9. On which toolbar is the Zoom list box located?

EXAM 1 PAGE 2

10. What function does the drag-and-drop pointer enable you to perform on the Slides tab?

11. Working in Slide Sorter view or on the Slides tab, how do you delete a slide without using the menu?

12. When running a slide show, how do you activate the pen pointer?

13. When running a slide show, what happens when you:

    A. Press N on the keyboard?

    B. Press the left arrow key?

    C. Click the left mouse button?

14. What do you click to display a shortcut menu?

15. Which keyboard command displays the Print dialog box?

16. If you have an 8-slide presentation, which print option do you choose to print scaled-down images of all slides on one page?

17. When viewing a slide in Normal view, with both the PowerPoint application window and the presentation window maximized:

    A. Where are the Close buttons located?

    B. Which Close button do you use to close the presentation?

18. List all available options for printing handouts (in terms of slides per page).

EXAM 1 PAGE 3

19. How do you access the AutoContent Wizard after PowerPoint is open?

20. How do you turn on the AutoCorrect feature?

21. When adding information to a presentation handout, where on the page are the following items inserted?

A. Date and time

B. Header

C. Footer

D. Page number

22. List two ways to start the spell-checker.

23. Name the three PowerPoint View buttons.
A.
B.
C.

NAME: ______________________ CLASS: ______________________

Exam 1

Applications

Create a presentation about employee orientation.

1. Use the AutoContent Wizard to create an on-screen presentation, using the presentation type Employee Orientation (from the Corporate category). Use the title **Welcome New Employees**. In the slide footer, include the text **Prepared by** followed by your name. Include the slide number on all slides, but not the date.
2. Change the subtitle to **Good 4 U**
3. On slide 2, delete the following bulleted items *and then* delete the slides with the same titles:
   - ♦ History of company & company vision
   - ♦ Company policies
   - ♦ Required paperwork
   - ♦ Summary
4. On slide 2, move “Performance reviews” before “Benefits review.” Reorder the slides with the same titles.
5. On slide 3 (“Who’s Who”), replace the existing bullets with the following three bulleted items:
   - ♦ **Gus Irvinelli and Julie Wolfe, Co-owners**
   - ♦ **Michele Jenkins, Head Chef**
   - ♦ **Roy Olafsen, Marketing Manager**
6. On slide 4 (“Performance Reviews”), replace the existing bulleted items with the following three:
   - ♦ **Purpose: Salary increase/promotion**
   - ♦ **Frequency: Every six months**
   - ♦ **The review process**
7. On slide 5 (“Benefits Review”), delete the last two bulleted items.
8. On slide 6 (“Other Resources”), change the last two bulleted items to the following:
   - ♦ **Weekly lunch meetings**
   - ♦ **Monthly training sessions**
9. Apply the Newsflash transition effect at slow speed to all slides.
10. Check spelling in the presentation.
11. Add a handout header that contains your name, and a handout footer with the text ***[your initials]*Exam1**. Include today’s date as a fixed date.
12. Save the presentation as ***[your initials]*Exam1** in a new folder for Exam1.
13. Print as handouts, 6 slides per page, pure black-and-white, framed.
14. Close the presentation.

NAME: ____________________ CLASS: ____________________

Exam 2

Questions

Answer the following questions. You can use your computer during the exam. Remember to monitor the amount of time remaining in the period.

1. Which keyboard combination is used to undo an action?

2. In the Outline tab, what shape is the pointer when it is placed over a slide icon?

3. In the Outline tab, what shape is the pointer when it is placed over a bullet?

4. To create a PowerPoint presentation from a Word outline, what commands do you choose?

5. When you create a new presentation, which slide layout is generally used for the first slide?

6. What shortcut key combination can you use to convert selected text into a hyperlink?

7. What are the three elements included in the Title and 2-Column Text slide layout?

8. After you key the last bulleted item on a Title and Text slide, which keyboard command can you use to add a new slide to the presentation?

EXAM 2 PAGE 2

9. Which two buttons on the Formatting toolbar can you use to change bullet levels?

10. How do you use the status bar to change the design template?

11. Which toolbar contains the Redo button?

12. Summary slides are created from which slide component?

13. On the Outlining toolbar, which button do you use to display only title text for all slides?

14. On the Outlining toolbar, which two buttons can you use to move slides?

15. List the keyboard shortcut for each of the following functions:

A. Underline text

B. Make text bold

C. Increase font size

D. Right-align text

16. Which tab in the Format Placeholder dialog box is used to make a placeholder smaller?

17. How do you display the Picture Bullet dialog box?

18. What shape is the pointer when you're resizing a placeholder by dragging one of its sizing handles?

EXAM 2 PAGE 3

19. How do you use the menu to display the slide master?

20. On the title master, which placeholder appears below the title placeholder?

21. Which key can you press to deselect a placeholder?

22. How do you use the menu to execute the Repeat command?

NAME: ____________________________ CLASS: ____________________________

Exam 2

Applications

Create a presentation that describes mistakes commonly made when writing a resume.

1. Open the presentation **ResForms** from your student disk. Save it as ***[your initials]*****ResForms** in a new folder for Exam 2 and then close it. (You will create a hyperlink to this file later.)
2. Start a blank presentation. On the title slide, key **Ten Common Mistakes in Writing a Resume** as the title and your name as the subtitle.
3. Apply the design template **Profile** and change to the color scheme with the medium blue background.
4. Use the slide master to change the title font to 40-point Arial Black. Use the title master to change the title to 48-point Arial Black.
5. On slide 1, drag the subtitle placeholder so that your name appears centered horizontally.
6. Insert a new slide as slide 2, using the Title and Text slide layout. Key the title **Ten Top Resume Mistakes**
7. In the Outline tab, key the following bulleted items under the slide 2 title:
   - **Gimmicky**
   - **Sloppy presentation**
   - **Poor organization**
   - **Unrealistic goal**
   - **Not tailored to employer or job**
   - **Best features not emphasized**
   - **Vague about details**
   - **Exaggerated information**
   - **Irrelevant information included**
   - **Wordy**
8. Using the Outline tab, move "Gimmicky" to the bottom of the list (below "Wordy") and move "Wordy" up one line (below "Exaggerated information").
9. Divide slide 2 into three slides, all with the title "Top Ten Resume Mistakes." Slide 2 should contain the first four bulleted items. Slide 3 should contain the two bullets "Best features not emphasized" and "Vague about details." Slide 4 should contain the remaining four bulleted items.
10. On slide 3, under "Vague about details," key the following second-level bulleted items:
    - **When?**
    - **Who?**

EXAM 2 PAGE 5

- **What?**

11. On slides 2–4, add numbers before each first-level bulleted item (key the number, period, and space character). For example, the first bullet on slide 1 should appear as:

    ▪ **1. Sloppy presentation**

12. Check spelling in the presentation.
13. On slide 2, use the text "Poor organization" to create a hyperlink to the file ***[your initials]*****ResForms**.
14. On the handouts, include the date and your name as the header and include the page number and the text ***[your initials]*****Exam2** as the footer.
15. Save the presentation as ***[your initials]*****Exam2** in your Exam 2 folder.
16. View the presentation as a slide show, testing the hyperlink on slide 2.
17. Print as handouts, 4 slides per page, grayscale, framed.
18. Close the presentation.

NAME: ____________________________ CLASS: ___________________________

Exam 3

Questions

Answer the following questions. You can use your computer during the exam. Remember to monitor the amount of time remaining in the period.

1. Identify the toolbar where each of the following appears:

   A. Save and Open buttons

   B. Font drop-down list

   C. Crop button

   D. 3-D button

2. Identify the menu commands you use to accomplish the following operations:

   A. Right-align text

   B. Display a master slide

   C. Create a PowerPoint table

   D. Change the case of selected text

   E. Replace fonts throughout a presentation

3. Name the keyboard command you use to accomplish the following operations:

   A. Select all objects on a slide

   B. Undo an action

   C. Duplicate an object

4. List two methods, using a toolbar, to change selected text to a larger font size.

   A.

   B.

EXAM 3 PAGE 2

5. Identify the Drawing toolbar button you use for the following operations:

   A. Add a patterned fill to an object

   B. Remove a border from an object

   C. Draw a star

   D. Draw a circle

   E. Change a text box border to a dotted line

6. After you click within a text placeholder, what does pressing the Escape key do?

7. List the menu commands and dialog box options needed to change the color of a bullet.

8. After replacing Times New Roman with Arial in a presentation, list two methods for restoring the font to Times New Roman:

   A.

   B.

9. Which slide layout contains a content placeholder on the right side of the slide?

10. Which sizing handles do you use to proportionately size a clip art object?

11. Which key must you press to draw a perfect square instead of a rectangle?

12. What shape is the pointer when you're performing the following operations?

    A. Dragging a sizing handle

    B. Drawing a text box

EXAM 3 PAGE 3

C. Drawing a rectangle

D. Dragging a text box

E. Rotating an object

F. Dragging an AutoShape adjustment handle

13. Which menu command removes a slide from a presentation?

14. Name the button, and the toolbar on which it is located, that you use to apply an arrowhead to the end of a line.

15. Name the menu command you use to change a star into a cube.

16. Which tab on the Fill Effects dialog box do you use to apply these fill effects?

A. White Marble

B. Early Sunset preset

C. Checkerboard

D. Granite

17. Describe one way to edit the text of a selected WordArt object.

18. Which button do you use to copy the formatting of one object to another object?

19. How do you change an object shadow's color?

20. Which tab in the Color Scheme dialog box do you use to perform the following functions?

    A. Choose a different predefined color scheme

    B. Change the background color only

    C. Delete a color scheme

    D. Add a new color scheme to the Standard color schemes

21. Explain the difference between a vector-based picture and a bitmap.

22. Describe a method for selecting three adjacent objects on a slide.

23. List the steps to change the black-and-white setting for a slide object.

24. Which action displays a dialog box that asks if you want to convert an object to a Microsoft Office drawing object?

EXAM 3 PAGE 5

NAME: ______________________ CLASS: ______________________

Exam 3

Applications

Create a presentation and work with text, clip art, drawing objects, and master slides.

1. Create the presentation shown in Figure 3-1 by using the default (blank) design template.

FIGURE 3-1

Slide 1:

Elements of a Good Presentation
[your name]

Slide 2:

Language and Content

- Use consistent wording
- Use brief wording
- Include a title slide and introductory slide
- Reflect purpose of presentation throughout

Slide 3:

Bulleted Text

- Bulleted items: No more than 7
- Words: No more than 7 per item
- Levels: No more than 2
- Text: No smaller than 24 points

Slide 4:

Color and Design

- Use PowerPoint's design templates
- Keep backgrounds simple
- Customize colors carefully

Slide 5:

Clip Art and Drawing Objects

- Keep to a minimum
- Size appropriately

- `Use clip art that relates to content`

2. Apply the **Edge** design template using the default color scheme.
3. On the slide master, change the title text to 44-point bold. Change the first-level bullet to a gold check mark (using the fills scheme color). Size the check mark appropriately.
4. On the title master, reduce the title text font size by one increment and make the subtitle text bold.
5. Replace the font Garamond with Verdana throughout the presentation and then replace Arial with Garamond.
6. On the slide master, find and insert a suitable clip art picture by using the search word "crayon."
7. Size the clip appropriately and move it to an attractive position in the lower-right corner of the slide.
8. On slide 1, delete the word "Presentation" in the title. Create a WordArt object of the word "Presentation" by choosing the fourth WordArt style in the third row and 44-point Verdana Bold for the font.
9. Change the WordArt shape to Wave 2 (the sixth shape in the third row) to make it curved.
10. Resize the WordArt object so that it blends well with the rest of the slide and center it below the title.
11. On slide 3, draw a 6-inch-wide text box at the bottom of the slide. In the text box, key **Note: There are always exceptions to these rules.** Use 24-point Monotype Corsiva (or another readable "handwritten" font).
12. Apply a two-color shaded fill to the text box by using the default colors (fills scheme color and background scheme color) shaded horizontally with the lighter color at the center. Change the transparency settings for the fill effect to 50%.
13. Center-align the text within the text box and position it attractively at the bottom of the slide.
14. Check spelling in the presentation.
15. On the handouts, include the date and your name as the header and include the page number and the text ***[your initials]*****Exam3** as the footer.
16. Save the presentation as ***[your initials]*****Exam3**.
17. Print as handouts, 6 slides per page, grayscale, framed.
18. Close the presentation.

NAME: ______________________ CLASS: ______________________

Exam 4

Questions

Answer the following questions. You can use your computer during the exam. Remember to monitor the amount of time remaining in the period.

1. How do you use the menu to display the ruler?

2. Which indent marker on the ruler do you use to set a first-line indent?

3. After drawing an AutoShape and keying text in the object, list the steps you follow to resize the selected object to accommodate the text without using the sizing handles.

4. How do you move a tab marker?

5. How do you delete a tab marker?

6. Describe or draw the symbol that identifies a center tab.

7. Which dialog box do you use to adjust the internal margins for a shape that contains text?

8. How do you save a presentation as a design template?

9. List the steps to open the Edit Color Scheme dialog box.

10. How many design templates can you use in a single presentation?

11. How would you set the amount of space before bulleted text paragraphs to 0.5 lines?

12. If you want to copy a presentation's color scheme and background to another presentation (but not the other design elements), what toolbar button must you use and from what type of object must you copy the color scheme?

13. If you disregard good taste, how many animations can you apply to a single object?

14. Where does the body text in a summary slide come from?

15. Name three types of objects that you can link to when using a hyperlink.

16. What is the Rehearse Timings command used for?

17. If you insert a sound clip on a slide, but you don't want to display its icon, where should you position it?

18. Which indent marker do you use to change the distance between bullets and text?

19. How do you access the dialog box in which you can change the page orientation of handouts?

EXAM 4 PAGE 3

20. How can you change the font size of the header and footer information to be printed on your presentation handouts?

21. Hidden slides do not appear in which view?

22. How do you change the order of animations on a slide?

23. How do you remove an animation effect from a slide without deleting the animated object?

24. Name the dialog box you use to create a custom toolbar.

25. Which command on the Slide Show menu can you use to add a link to a summary or agenda slide?

NAME: ______________________ CLASS: ______________________

Exam 4

Applications

Create a presentation that includes a tabbed table, custom animations, a drawing object, and a hyperlink to a hidden slide.

1. Open the file **JobFair4**.
2. Change the background to a horizontal gradient fill, using the Early Sunset preset with dark blue at the bottom.
3. Replace the Arial font with Tahoma throughout the presentation.
4. On the slide master, increase the text size in the title and body text placeholders by one increment and make the text bold.
5. On the slide master, apply the entrance animation effect Wipe, From Left, Medium speed to both the title and bulleted text placeholders. The title should appear first automatically and then each bulleted item should appear one at a time with a mouse click.
6. Still working on the slide master, apply a Diagonal Down gradient fill with the Fire preset color to the Good 4 U logo. Choose the sample with the brightest color in the upper-right corner.
7. Apply 3-D Style 1 to the Good 4 U logo and change the 3-D color to white. Reduce the depth of the 3-D effect to 24 points.
8. Apply the Spiral In entrance effect to the Good 4 U logo; then apply the emphasis effect Spin. The logo should appear on a mouse click, and the spin should play automatically as the logo appears. Both effects should be executed at medium speed.
9. Resize the Good 4 U logo proportionately to 4.25 inches wide and center it horizontally relative to the slide.
10. Insert a title master. (Tip: Use the Slide Master View toolbar.)
11. On the title master, move both text placeholders to the top half of the slide.
12. Resize the title master's Good 4 U logo proportionately to 8 inches wide. Position the logo attractively in the lower half of the title master and center it horizontally relative to the slide.
13. Change the layout of slide 3 to Title Slide.
14. Insert a new slide after slide 2, using the Title Only layout.
15. On the new slide, key the title **Starting Salaries** and create a tabbed table with the following text (insert tabs appropriately and use the same font size and format as the body text on slide 2):

    Waiter/Waitress $ 8.00 hr.
    Assistant Chef $ 12.50 hr.
    Experienced Chef $ 17.50 hr.
16. Hide the "Starting Salaries" slide.

17. On slide 2, insert an Information action button that hyperlinks to the hidden slide. Size the action button to 50% of its original size and position it in the lower-left corner.
18. Run the slide show and test your hyperlink.
19. Adjust grayscale settings as needed.
20. Check spelling in the presentation.
21. On the handouts, include the date and your name as the header and include the page number and the text ***[your initials]*Exam4** as the footer.
22. Save the presentation as ***[your initials]*Exam4**.
23. Print as handouts (including the hidden slide), 4 slides per page, landscape, grayscale, framed. Close the presentation.

NAME: ____________________ CLASS: ____________________

Exam 5

Questions

Answer the following questions. You can use your computer during the exam. Remember to monitor the amount of time remaining in the period.

1. When working in Microsoft Graph, in what window do you enter or edit chart data?

2. Which dialog box do you use to change the scale of the value axis on a chart?

3. Describe the toolbar method for changing a column chart to a pie chart.

4. Describe one way to delete a chart's legend.

5. Which characteristics define a chart that is:

   A. Selected but not activated?

   B. Selected and activated?

6. List two ways to insert a blank PowerPoint table on a slide without having to draw it:

   A.

   B.

7. How do you activate an existing chart for editing?

8. List the steps to change the arrangement of a group of subordinate boxes in an org chart so they are stacked vertically in one column.

9. If a yellow diamond appears on a connector line, what do you use it for?

10. When a connector line is selected, what does a green endpoint indicate?

11. List the steps to float the Connectors toolbar.

12. Which slide layout would you typically choose to create a slide with a flowchart?

13. What type of PowerPoint diagram is used to show a continuous process?

14. What feature needs to be turned off if you want to move one or more diagram shapes independently from the others?

15. After copying a Word table to the clipboard, which dialog box do you use to add the object to your current slide while preserving the ability to edit it by using Word features?

16. List two buttons on the Tables and Borders toolbar that enable you to merge cells:

    A.

    B.

EXAM 5 PAGE 3

17. On a chart, which button can you use to change the fill effect of a selected data series?

18. Which dialog box and tab are used to rotate a chart axis title?

19. How do you explode a slice of a pie chart?

20. When three columns in a PowerPoint table are selected, how do you make all three columns the same width?

EXAM 5 PAGE 4

NAME: ______________________ CLASS: ______________________

Exam 5

Applications

Create a presentation that includes a chart, a table, and a flowchart.

1. Start a new presentation and key the text for four slides, as shown in Figure 5-1.

FIGURE 5-1

Slide 1:

Title: Good *4 U* Herbal Teas

Subtitle: New Product Line

Slide 2:

Why Herbal Tea?

- Healthy alternative to coffee
- Delicious and refreshing
- Can be served hot or cold

Slide 3:

Current Customer Preferences

- Vanilla Spice herbal tea is the new best-selling beverage
- Iced and hot tea sales are equal
- Herbal tea now accounts for 40% of beverage sales

Slide 4:

Marketing Objectives

- Immediate

– Launch Vanilla Spice as prototype

– Design package and manufacture locally

– Sell at restaurant

- Future

EXAM 5 PAGE 5

- Market nationally within two years
- Develop product line

2. Apply the **Balloons** design template to the presentation. On the slide master, make the title bold and one size smaller.
3. On the slide master, create a WordArt logo with the text **Good 4 U Tea**. Choose the fifth style in the fourth row (the yellow curved text).
4. Change the border and fill of the WordArt object to your choice of a gradient fill by using colors from the presentation color scheme. Resize the WordArt object, making it 2.0 inches high by 4.5 inches wide.
5. Position the WordArt object in the lower-right corner of the slide.
6. Copy the WordArt to slide 1. Then resize and reposition it so that it harmonizes with the text on the slide.
7. Insert a new slide after slide 3, using the Title and Content layout. Key the title **Vanilla Spice Tea Tops the Charts**
8. Create a column chart by using the data shown in Figure 5-2. The data should display by row.

FIGURE 5-2

		A
		Weekly Sales Percentage
1	Vanilla Spice Tea	40
2	Sparkling Water	30
3	Juice	15
4	Coffee	10
5	Other	5

9. Position the legend above the chart and remove its border.
10. Adjust the size and position of the chart so that it does not conflict with the WordArt.
11. Custom-animate the chart so it appears one bar at a time, automatically by series with the Chime sound effect.
12. Add a new slide after the chart slide, using the Title and Content layout. Key the title **Vanilla Spice: The Crowd Pleaser**, reduce its font size by one increment, and adjust the size of the title placeholder so that the title does not word wrap.
13. Create a table by using the data shown in Figure 5-2.
14. For the cells with numbers, set a 1.8-inch internal right margin and right-align the text. Remove the table borders.
15. Merge the table cells in the first row and center its text. Adjust the table's size and position so that it does not conflict with the WordArt in the lower-right corner.

Exams

16. Insert a new slide after slide 5, using the Title Only layout. Key the title **Herbal Tea Goals**
17. Create a radial diagram on slide 5. Key the text **Profitable Product Line** on three lines in the center circle and the following in the surrounding circles, each word on a separate line:
    12 o'clock circle: **Customer Recognition**
    4 o'clock circle: **Repeat Sales**
    8 o'clock circle: **Create Retail Market**
18. Scale the diagram, making it as large as possible without overlapping other slide elements.
19. Change all the diagram text to 18-point Arial Narrow.
20. Format the connecting lines with arrows pointing toward the center circle.
21. Change fills and line colors in the diagram to create a pleasing effect.
22. Apply a transition effect of your choice to all slides in the presentation, advancing to the next slide manually.
23. Run the slide show to check your transitions and animation settings.
24. Check spelling and grayscale settings in the presentation.
25. On the handouts, include the date and your name as the header and include the page number and the text ***[your initials]*****Exam5** as the footer.
26. Save the presentation as ***[your initials]*****Exam5**.
27. Print as handouts, 4 slides per page, landscape, grayscale, framed. Close the presentation.

NAME: ____________________ CLASS: ____________________

Exam 6

Questions

Answer the following questions. You can use your computer during the exam. Remember to monitor the amount of time remaining in the period.

1. What type of software enables you to view Web pages?

2. When you export meeting minutes to Word, the document that is created is in what file format?

3. What size are slides that are formatted for an on-screen presentation?

4. What type of slide orientation is taller than it is wide?

5. Which menu command enables you to see how a presentation will appear as a Web page without first saving it as a Web page?

6. What happens to your presentation's animation effects when you deliver your presentation by using 35mm slides?

7. What PowerPoint feature can you use to save a large presentation to floppy disks?

8. When working in Slide view, which menu can you use to open the Meeting Minder dialog box?

9. Name the file that you must run to unpack a Pack and Go presentation.

10. For what reason might you want to embed fonts in a presentation when you save it?

11. What can you do to see what a presentation will look like as a Web page before you save it in HTML format?

12. What is the first page you see when you use a browser to play a presentation broadcast?

13. To deliver a presentation on an overhead projector, on what medium do you print your slides?

14. If you receive one or more files that are reviews of your presentation, how do you combine the files so that you can see all the suggested changes at the same time?

15. How can you print a list of comments that have been added to a presentation?

EXAM 6 PAGE 3

NAME: ____________________ CLASS: ____________________

Exam 6

Applications

Merge presentations from multiple reviewers, accept and reject changes, insert comments, and print comments.

1. Open the file **RetR1** and insert the following comments:
   On slide 1: **I added the Good 4 U Logo. I hope you don't think it is too busy.**
   On slide 2: **I simplified the wording for the second bullet.**
   On slide 3: **I simplified the wording here too because I thought there was too much on this slide.**
2. Save the presentation as ***[your initials]*exam6a** and close it. Do not print it.
3. Open the file **RetOrig** and then merge the file ***[your initials]*exam6a** with it.
4. On slide 1, accept the changes to the title and accept the insertion of the Good 4 U logo. Reject the changes to the subtitle text.
5. On slides 2 and 3, accept the bullet color changes but reject the text changes.
6. On slide 4, accept all the changes; then end the review.
7. Run a slide show and insert the Meeting Minder minutes and action items described in Figure 6-1.

FIGURE 6-1

Meeting Minutes:

The marketing department reviewed the Good 4 U Retreats presentation on January 2nd.

Everyone present at the meeting agreed that the retreat program is a good one, and that it should be expanded for 2003.

Roy Olafsen asked several staff members to present a plan for a new retreat to be included next year.

Action Items:

Marie Jones is to present a plan for a retreat to take place in March, 2003. Her presentation is due on 4/15/2002.

Carla Frank is to present a plan for a retreat to take place in August, 2003. Her presentation is due on 4/18/2002.

John Brinks is to present a plan for a retreat to take place

```
in May, 2003. His presentation is due on 4/20/2002.
```

8. Export the meeting minutes and action items to Word. Insert your name at the top of the document and save it as a Word file with the filename **Exam6b**.
9. Print the Word document and then close it.
10. Edit the action slide so that the text is easy to read. You can make changes to the layout if you think it will make the slide more attractive.
11. Create a handout header and footer: include the date and your name as the header, and the page number and text ***[your initials]*****Exam6c** as the footer.
12. Save the presentation as ***[your initials]*****Exam6c**.
13. Print the presentation comments and handouts, 6 slides per page, landscape, grayscale, framed. Close the presentation.

EXAM 1 KEY PAGE 1

Exam 1 KEY

Questions

1. Standard and Formatting toolbars
2. At the bottom left corner, above the status bar (or above the Drawing toolbar).
3. A possible style error is being identified.
4. Position arrow pointer over a toolbar button.
5. I-beam
6. Arrow
7. Advance to (or display) the next slide.
8. Print button
9. Standard
10. Move slides (change the order of slides).
11. Click the slide to select it, and then press the Delete key.
12. Open shortcut menu, choose Pointer Options, Pen.
13. A. Display the next slide.
    B. Display the previous slide.
    C. Display the next slide.
14. Click right mouse button.
15. Ctrl+P
16. Handouts (9 slides per page)
17. A. Upper right corner of the screen
    B. Bottom Close button
18. 1, 2, 3, 4, 6, and 9 slides per page
19. Choose New from the File menu, then choose From AutoContent Wizard on the New Presentation task pane.
20. Choose AutoCorrect from the Tools menu and check Replace Text As You Type.
21. A. Upper right
    B. Upper left
    C. Lower left
    D. Lower right
22. Click Spelling button, press F7, or choose Spelling from the Tools menu.
23. A. Normal view
    B. Slide Sorter view
    C. Slide Show

Exam 2 KEY

Questions

1. Ctrl+Z
2. Four-pointed arrow
3. Four-pointed arrow
4. Insert, Slides form Outline.
5. Title Slide
6. [Ctrl]+[K]
7. Two body text placeholders (left and right) and a title placeholder.
8. Ctrl+M or Ctrl+Enter
9. Increase Indent and Decrease Indent
10. Double-click the current design template name that is displayed on the status bar.
11. Standard
12. Slide title
13. Collapse All
14. Move Up and Move Down buttons
15. A. Ctrl+U
    B. Ctrl+B
    C. Ctrl+Shift+>
    D. Ctrl+R
16. Size tab
17. Open Bullets and Numbering dialog box, click the Bulleted tab, then click Picture.
18. Two-pointed arrow
19. Click View, Master, Slide Master
20. Subtitle placeholder
21. Esc key
22. Edit, Repeat

Exam 3 KEY

Questions

1. A. Standard toolbar
   B. Formatting toolbar
   C. Picture toolbar
   D. Drawing toolbar
2. A. Format, Alignment, Align Right
   B. View, Master
   C. Insert, Table
   D. Format, Change Case
   E. Format, Replace Fonts
3. A. Ctrl+A
   B. Ctrl+Z
   C. Ctrl+D
4. A. On the Formatting toolbar, use the Font Size drop-down list.
   B. Use the Increase Font Size button.
5. A. Fill Color
   B. Line Color
   C. AutoShapes
   D. Oval
   E. Dash Style
6. Select the placeholder border.
7. Choose Format, Bullets and Numbering, Color drop-down list.
8. A. Choose Undo.
   B. Use the Replace Fonts command from the Format menu.
9. Title, Text, and Content layout
10. Any corner handle
11. Shift key
12. A. Two-headed arrow
    B. Cross
    C. Cross
    D. Four-headed arrow
    E. Circling arrows
    F. Small arrowhead
13. Edit, Delete Slide
14. Arrow Style button on Drawing toolbar
15. Draw, Change AutoShape
16. A. Texture
    B. Gradient
    C. Pattern
    D. Texture
17. Click the Edit Text button on the WordArt toolbar, or choose Edit Text on the shortcut menu, choose Text from the Edit menu, or double-click the WordArt object.
18. Format Painter

EXAM 3 KEY PAGE 2

19. Select the object, click the Shadow Style button and choose Shadow Settings from the list box. On the Shadow settings toolbar, click the Shadow Color list box arrow and choose a new color.
20. A. Standard tab
    B. Custom tab
    C. Standard tab
    D. Custom tab
21. A bitmap is made up of many tiny dots. When you scale it, it can become blurred. A vector picture is made up of an arrangement of lines and shapes. When you scale it, it retains its detail.
22. Hold Shift key and click each object, or draw a selection rectangle around the objects.
23. From the View menu, choose Color/Grayscale, Grayscale; or click the Grayscale button on the Standard toolbar and choose Grayscale. Select the object to be changed, then choose a setting from the Setting list box on the Grayscale View toolbar.
24. Ungroup a clip art image.

Exam 4 KEY

Questions
1. Choose View, Ruler.
2. Top indent marker (top triangle)
3. Choose Format, AutoShape; click Text Box tab; check Resize AutoShape to fit text.
4. Drag it along the ruler to the new position.
5. Drag it off the ruler (in any direction).
6. An upside-down "T"
7. Format AutoShape, Text Box
8. Choose File, Save As, and then choose Design Template from the Save as type list box.
9. Display the Slide Design task pane, choose Color Schemes from the task pane, then choose Edit Color Scheme from the bottom of the task pane.
10. As many design templates as there are slides in the presentation (less if you want your presentation to display good taste).
11. Choose Format, Line Spacing, and set the Before Paragraph setting to 0.5 lines.
12. Format Painter button, master slide thumbnail
13. As many as you want
14. The titles of the slides you choose when you create the summary slide
15. Web page, PowerPoint slide in current presentation, a different PowerPoint presentation, a video file, an Excel spreadsheet, a Word document, etc.
16. To set slides to advance automatically after an appropriate amount of time.
17. Beyond the slide's border or; in the gray area surrounding the slide.
18. Left indent marker (bottom triangle)
19. File, Page Setup
20. Display the Handout Master, select each area, and change the font size.
21. Slide Show
22. In the custom animations list on the Custom Animation task pane, drag an animation list item up or down to a new position.
23. Right-click the item in the custom animation list and choose Remove or; Select the animation item in the custom animation list and press Delete.
24. Customize
25. Action Buttons

Exam 5 KEY

Questions

1. Datasheet
2. Format Axis
3. Click the Chart Type button arrow and choose Pie from the drop-down list.
4. Click the Legend button on the Microsoft Graph Standard toolbar; Select the legend and press Delete; right-click the legend and choose Clear.
5. A. White sizing handles.
   B. Black sizing handles, diagonal line border, and Microsoft Graph menu and toolbars.
6. Students may choose two of the following three answers:
   A. Click the Insert Table button on the Standard toolbar.
   B. Choose a Content slide layout and click its Insert Table icon.
   C. Choose Table from the Insert menu.
7. Double-click the organization chart.
8. Select the group's superior box, then click the Layout list box arrow on the Organization Chart tool bar, then select Left Hanging or Right Hanging.
9. Change the connector's shape.
10. The green endpoint is not locked onto (connected to) an AutoShape.
11. Click AutoShapes, Connectors, and drag the submenu's gray title bar.
12. Title Only or Blank
13. Cycle diagram.
14. Turn off AutoLayout.
15. Paste Special
16. A. Merge Cells button
    B. Eraser button
17. Fill Color
18. Format Axis Title dialog box, Alignment tab
19. Select the slice and then drag it away from the center of the pie.
20. Click the Distribute Columns Evenly button on the Tables and Borders toolbar.

Exam 6 KEY

Questions

1. Browser
2. Rich Text Format (.rtf)
3. 10 by 7.5 inches
4. Portrait
5. File menu, Web Page Preview
6. The animations are lost. Animations can only be displayed when the slide show is run from a computer.
7. Pack and Go
8. Tools menu
9. Pngsetup.exe
10. To make sure that the original fonts are used when the presentation is run on a different computer.
11. From the File menu, choose Web Page Preview.
12. Lobby page
13. Transparency film.
14. From the Tools menu choose Compare and Merge Presentations, then in the dialog box choose the files to be merged.
15. When printing one or more slides, handouts, or notes pages, check the Include Comment Pages check box on the Print dialog box.

Student Name 1/28/02

Welcome New Employees

Good 4 U

Prepared by Student Name 1

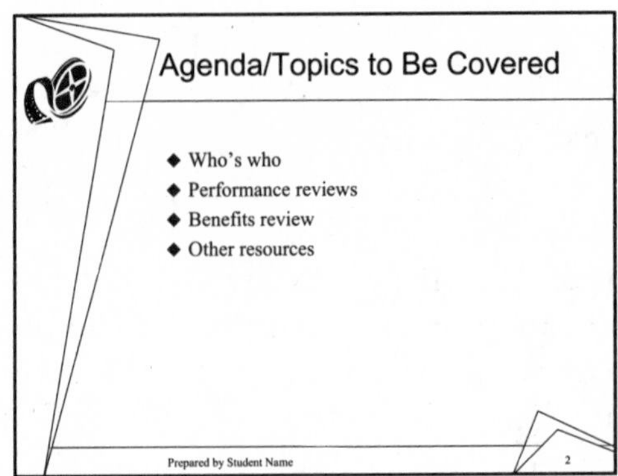

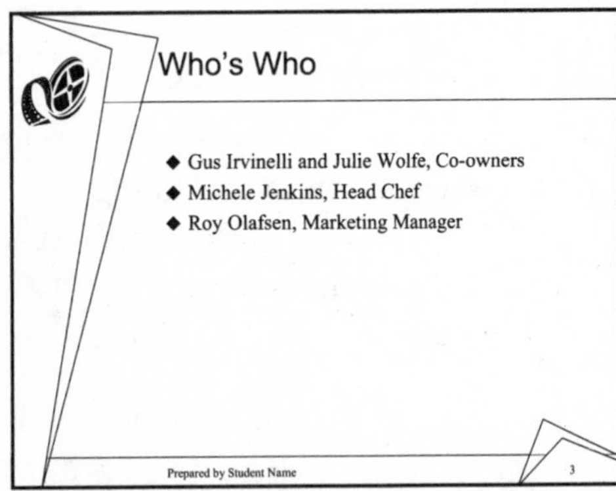

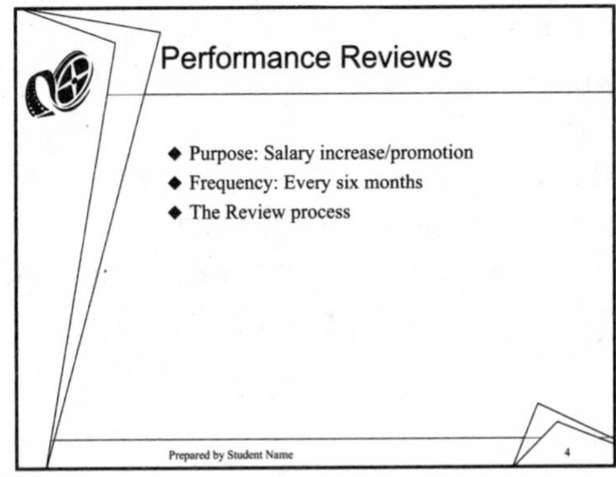

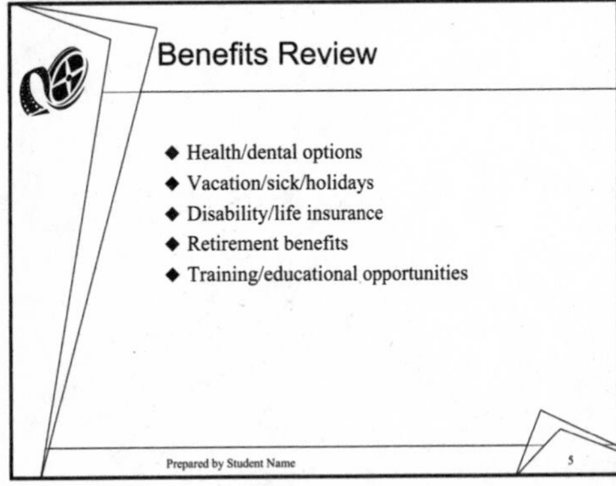

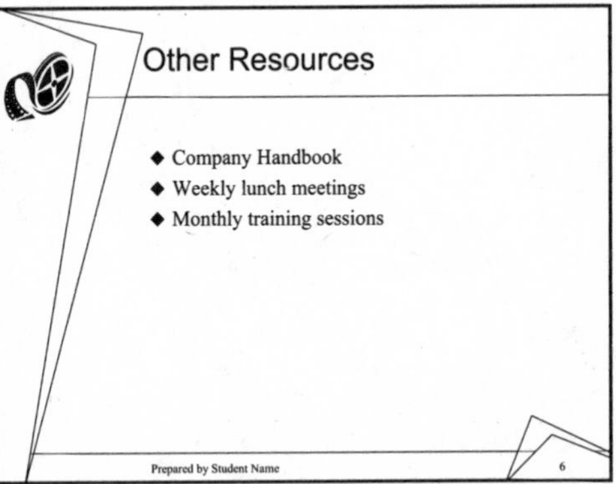

Exam1

Exam1

Student Name 1/28/02

Ten Common Mistakes in Writing a Resume

Student Name

Ten Top Resume Mistakes

- ☐ 1. Sloppy presentation
- ☐ 2. Poor organization
- ☐ 3. Unrealistic goal
- ☐ 4. Not tailored to employer or job

Ten Top Resume Mistakes

- ☐ 5. Best features not emphasized
- ☐ 6. Vague about details
  - ■ When?
  - ■ Who?
  - ■ What?

Ten Top Resume Mistakes

- ☐ 7. Exaggerated information
- ☐ 8. Wordy
- ☐ 9. Irrelevant information included
- ☐ 10. Gimmicky

Exam2 1

Student Name 1/28/02

Elements of a Good Presentation

Student Name

Language and Content

- Use consistent wording
- Use brief wording
- Include a title slide and introductory slide
- Reflect purpose of presentation throughout

Bulleted Text

- Bulleted items: No more than 7
- Words: No more than 7 per item
- Levels: No more than 2
- Text: No smaller than 24 points

Note: There are always exceptions to these rules.

Color and Design

- Use PowerPoint's design templates
- Keep backgrounds simple
- Customize colors carefully

Clip Art and Drawing Objects

- Keep to a minimum
- Size appropriately
- Use clip art that relates to content

Exam3

Student Name 1/28/02

Great Jobs 4 U

At New York's Favorite Healthy Restaurant

Good 4 U is Looking For

- **Experienced waiters and waitresses**
- **Trained, creative chefs**
- **Assistant chefs: If you're willing to learn, we're willing to train you!**

Starting Salaries

Waiter/Waitress	$ 8.00 hr.
Assistant Chef	$ 12.50 hr.
Experienced Chef	$ 17.50 hr.

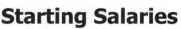

Interested?

Come talk to us at

Exam4 1

Exam4

Student Name 1/28/02

Good 4 U Herbal Teas

New Product Line

Good 4 U Tea

Why Herbal Tea?

- Healthy alternative to coffee
- Delicious and refreshing
- Can be served hot or cold

Good 4 U Tea

Current Customer Preferences

- Vanilla Spice herbal tea is the new best-selling beverage
- Iced and hot tea sales are equal
- Herbal tea now accounts for 40% of beverage sales

Good 4 U Tea

Vanilla Spice Tea Tops the Charts

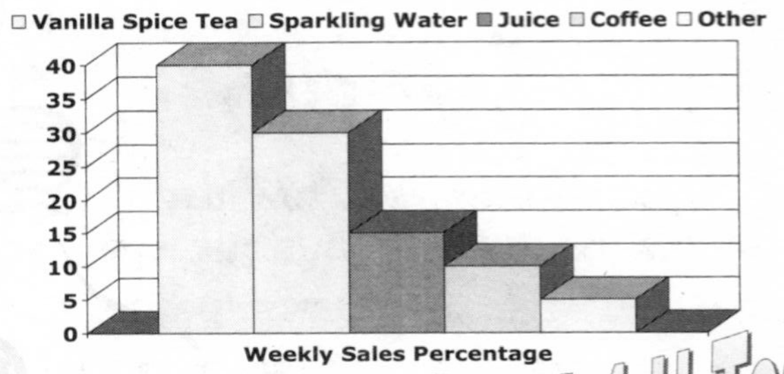

Vanilla Spice Tea
Sparkling Water
Juice
Coffee
Other

40
35
30
25
20
15
10
5
0

Weekly Sales Percentage

Good 4 U Tea

Exam5 1

Exam5 (page 1)

Student Name 1/28/02

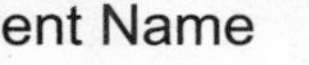

Vanilla Spice: The Crowd Pleaser

Weekly Sales Percentage	
Vanilla Spice Tea	40
Sparkling Water	30
Juice	15
Coffee	10
Other	5

Good 4 U Tea

Herbal Tea Goals

Customer Recognition

Profitable Product Line

Create Retail Market

Repeat Sales

Good 4 U Tea

Marketing Objectives

- Immediate
  - Launch Vanilla Spice as prototype
  - Design package and manufacture locally
  - Sell at restaurant
- Future
  - Market nationally within two years
  - Develop product line

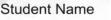

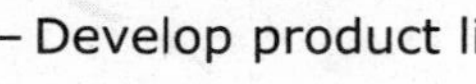

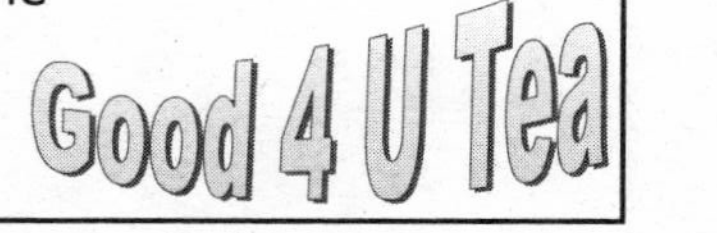

Exam5 2

Student Name
Meeting Minutes 1/27/2002 9:55 PM

RetOrig

Meeting Minutes

The marketing department reviewed the Good 4 U Retreats presentation on January 2nd.

Everyone present at the meeting agreed that the Retreat program is a good one, and that it should be expanded for 2003.

Roy Olafsen asked several staff members to present a plan for a new retreat to be included next year.

Action Items

Owner	Due Date	Description
Marie Jones	4/15/2002	Present a plan for a retreat to be held in March, 2003
Carla Frank	4/18/2002	Present a plan for a retreat to be held in August, 2003
John Brinks	4/20/2002	Present a plan for a retreat to take place in May, 2003.

Exam6b

R11

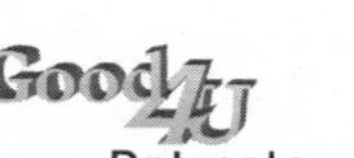

Retreats

Healthy Get-aways to regenerate your energy and creativity

R12

What is a Good 4 U Retreat?

- A mini vacation
- An opportunity to unwind in a healthy atmosphere
- Reinforcement for your healthy lifestyle

R13

Retreat features

- First class accommodations
- Healthy food with gourmet flair
- Slow-paced meditative nature walks
- Guided bicycle tours (all ability levels)
- Evening lectures on sports physiology and nutrition

2002 Retreat Schedule

March 22-25
  Florida's Keys
July 4-7
  Washington's San Juan Islands
October 4-7
  Vermont's Northeast Kingdom
November 8-11
  Utah's Canyonlands

Action Items

Owner	Due Date	Description
Marie Jones	4/15/2002	Present a plan for a retreat to be held in March, 2003
Carla Frank	4/18/2002	Present a plan for a retreat to be held in August, 2003
John Brinks	4/20/2002	Present a plan for a retreat to take place in May, 2003.

Exam6c

Slide 1

R11 I added the Good 4 U Logo. I hope you don't think its too busy.
Reviewer 1, 1/27/2002

Slide 2

R12 I simplified the wording for the second bullet.
Reviewer 1, 1/27/2002

Slide 3

R13 I simplified the wording here too because I thought there was too much on this slide.
Reviewer 1, 1/27/2002

Exam6c (comments)

EXAM 1 – ASSESSMENT CHECKLIST
Marple, *PowerPoint 2002*

EXAM 1
This exam is offered in two parts – "Questions" and "Applications." Testing time for each is 45 minutes. Each has a total of 100 possible points. You have the choice of administering one, or both, of the parts. If both parts are given, the point value for each Question and for each Applications step is one-half the point value stated below.

Coverage
Lessons 1 and 2

Questions

Question Number	Point Value	Comments
1	4	
2	4	
3	4	
4	4	
5	4	
6	4	
7	4	
8	4	
9	4	
10	4	
11	4	
12	4	
13	6	2 points per answer
14	4	
15	4	
16	4	
17	4	2 points per answer
18	4	
19	4	
20	4	
21	8	2 points per answer
22	4	
23	6	2 points per answer

Assessment Guide
Total points = 100

Applications

Applications Step	Point Value	Comments
1	25	Create new presentation using AutoContent Wizard
2	4	Edit subtitle
3	10	Delete text and slides
4	10	Move text and slides
5	5	Key text
6	5	Key text
7	5	Delete text
8	5	Key text
9	5	Add a transition effect
10	5	Spell check
11	10	Add handout header and footer
12	5	Save presentation
13	6	Print handouts
14	0	

Assessment Guide

Total points = 100

EXAM 2 – ASSESSMENT CHECKLIST

Marple, *PowerPoint 2002*

EXAM 2

This exam is offered in two parts – "Questions" and "Applications." Testing time for each is 45 minutes. Each has a total of 100 possible points. You have the choice of administering one, or both, of the parts. If both parts are given, the point value for each Question and for each Applications step is one-half the point value stated below.

Coverage

Lessons 3 through 5

Questions

Question Number	Point Value	Comments
1	4	
2	4	
3	4	
4	4	
5	4	
6	4	
7	4	
8	4	
9	4	
10	4	
11	4	
12	4	
13	4	
14	4	
15	16	4 points per answer
16	4	
17	4	
18	4	
19	4	
20	4	
21	4	
22	4	

Assessment Guide

Total points = 100

Applications

Applications Step	Point Value	Comments
1	1	Open a file and save it in Exam2 folder
2	10	Start blank presentation and enter title slide information
3	5	Apply design template
4	4	2 points for each master slide change
5	4	Align placeholder
6	5	Insert a new slide
7	12	Key text
8	6	3 points per move
9	10	5 points per correct set up of slides 3 and 4
10	8	Key subtext
11	8	Key numbers
12	5	Check spelling
13	4	Create a hyperlink
14	6	Apply headers and footer to handouts
15	4	Save presentation
16	4	View as slide show and test the hyperlink
17	4	Print handouts
18	0	

Assessment Guide

Total points = 100

EXAM 3 – ASSESSMENT CHECKLIST

Marple, *PowerPoint 2002*

EXAM 3

This exam is offered in two parts – "Questions" and "Applications." Testing time for each is 45 minutes. Each has a total of 100 possible points. You have the choice of administering one, or both, of the parts. If both parts are given, the point value for each Question and for each Applications step is one-half the point value stated below.

Coverage

Lessons 6 through 8

Questions

Question Number	Point Value	Comments
1	8	2 points per answer
2	10	2 points per answer
3	6	2 points per answer
4	4	2 points per answer
5	10	2 points per answer
6	2	
7	2	
8	4	2 points per answer
9	2	
10	2	
11	2	
12	12	2 points per answer
13	2	
14	2	
15	2	
16	8	2 points per answer
17	2	
18	2	
19	2	
20	8	2 points per answer
21	2	
22	2	
23	2	
24	2	

Assessment Guide

Total points = 100

Applications

Applications Step	Point Value	Comments
1	18	Key presentation
2	4	Apply design template
3	8	Make changes to slide master, 4 points per change
4	8	Make changes to title master, 4 points per change
5	6	Replace two fonts with two others, 3 points per change
6	5	Insert clip art on slide master
7	5	Size and position clip art
8	10	Create WordArt object
9	6	Change shape of WordArt object
10	6	Change size and position of WordArt object
11	6	Key text in a text box and format it.
12	5	Apply a fill effect to a text box.
13	4	Center align text in a text box and center the box on the slide.
14	3	Check Spelling.
15	2	Create handout headers and footers
16	2	Save the presentation
17	2	Print the handout
18	0	Close the presentation

Assessment Guide

Total points = 100

EXAM 4 – ASSESSMENT CHECKLIST

Marple, *PowerPoint 2002*

EXAM 4

This exam is offered in two parts – "Questions" and "Applications." Testing time for each is 45 minutes. Each has a total of 100 possible points. You have the choice of administering one, or both, of the parts. If both parts are given, the point value for each Question and for each Applications step is one-half the point value stated below.

Coverage

Lessons 9 through 11

Questions

Question Number	Point Value	Comments
1	4	
2	4	
3	4	
4	4	
5	4	
6	4	
7	4	
8	4	
9	4	
10	4	
11	4	
12	4	
13	4	
14	4	
15	4	
16	4	
17	4	
18	4	
19	4	
20	4	
21	4	
22	4	
23	4	
24	4	
25	4	

Assessment Guide

Total points = 100

Applications

Applications Step	Point Value	Comments
1	0	Open a file
2	3	Change background
3	4	Replace fonts
4	3	Change text size on slide master
5	11	Apply animation effects to text
6	4	Apply gradient fill to object
7	8	Apply and modify 3-D effect
8	11	Apply two animation effects to one object
9	3	Resize and center an object
10	4	Insert a title master
11	4	Rearrange placeholders on title master
12	4	Resize and reposition an animated object on title master
13	3	Change the slide layout for slide 3
14	3	Insert a new slide.
15	11	Create a tabbed table.
16	4	Hide a slide
17	6	Create action button hyperlink to hidden slide
18	3	Test hyperlink by running slide show.
19	3	Adjust grayscale settings
20	2	Check spelling
21	2	Insert handout header and footer
22	2	Save the presentation
23	2	Print presentation handouts.
	100	

Assessment Guide

Total points = 100

EXAM 5 – ASSESSMENT CHECKLIST

Marple, *PowerPoint 2002*

EXAM 5

This exam is offered in two parts – "Questions" and "Applications." Testing time for each is 45 minutes. Each has a total of 100 possible points. You have the choice of administering one, or both, of the parts. If both parts are given, the point value for each Question and for each Applications step is one-half the point value stated below.

Coverage

Lessons 12 through 14

Questions

Question Number	Point Value	Comments
1	5	
2	5	
3	5	
4	5	
5	5	
6	5	
7	5	
8	5	
9	5	
10	5	
11	5	
12	5	
13	5	
14	5	
15	5	
16	5	
17	5	
18	5	
19	5	
20	5	

Assessment Guide

Total points = 100

Applications

Applications Step	Point Value	Comments
1	8	Key presentation
2	3	Apply design template and make slide master changes
3	6	Create WordArt logo
4	3	Format and resize WordArt logo
5	2	Position WordArt logo
6	3	Copy WordArt, then resize and reposition it
7	3	Insert new slide and key title
8	5	Create Column chart
9	3	Format and position chart legend
10	3	Adjust size and position of finished chart
11	6	Apply custom animation to chart
12	4	Create new slide, key title, and change title font size
13	5	Create a PowerPoint table
14	4	Change internal margins and text alignment for table cells
15	3	Merge table cells and align text
16	3	Insert new slide and key title
17	5	Create Radial diagram and key text in its shapes
18	3	Resize the diagram
19	3	Change the diagram text font and text size
20	4	Format diagram lines
21	3	Change diagram's fill and line colors
22	4	Apply transition effect to all slides
23	5	Run slide show, check transitions and animation
24	3	Check spelling anal grayscale settings
25	2	Add handout header and footer
26	2	Save the presentation
27	2	Print presentation handouts, close presentation

Assessment Guide

Total points = 100

EXAM 6 – ASSESSMENT CHECKLIST

Marple, *PowerPoint 2002*

EXAM 6

This exam is offered in two parts – "Questions" and "Applications." Testing time for each is 45 minutes. Each has a total of 100 possible points. You have the choice of administering one, or both, of the parts. If both parts are given, the point value for each Question and for each Applications step is one-half the point value stated below.

Coverage

Lesson 15

Questions

Question Number	Point Value	Comments
1	6	
2	7	
3	7	
4	6	
5	7	
6	7	
7	7	
8	7	
9	7	
10	7	
11	6	
12	7	
13	6	
14	7	
15	6	

Assessment Guide

Total points = 100

Applications

Applications Step	Point Value	Comments
1	11	Open a presentation and add comments to three slides
2	2	Save and close the presentation
3	11	Open a different presentation and merge the saved one with it.
4	8	Accept and reject changes on slide 1
5	16	Accept and reject changes on slides 2 and 3
6	10	Accept all changes on slide 4 and end the review session
7	12	Run a slide show and record minutes and action items
8	8	Export minutes and action items to Word and save as a Word document.
9	4	Print the Word document and close it..
10	7	Make changes to the action item slide so it can be easily read.
11	3	Create handout header and footer
12	2	Save the presentation
13	6	Print the presentation as handouts and print comments.
	100	

Assessment Guide

Total points = 100